PRICING AND PERFORMANCE OF INITIAL PUBLIC OFFERINGS IN THE UNITED STATES

By the Same Author
(As Arabinda Ghosh)

OPEC, the Petroleum Industry, and United States
Energy Policy

Competition and Diversification in the
United States Petroleum Industry

Redefining Excellence:
The Financial Performance of
America's "Best-Run" Companies

PRICING AND PERFORMANCE OF INITIAL PUBLIC OFFERINGS IN THE UNITED STATES

ARVIN GHOSH

TRANSACTION PUBLISHERS
NEW BRUNSWICK (U.S.A.) AND LONDON (U.K.)

Library of Congress Catalog Number: 2006040426
ISBN: 0-7658-0326-7
Printed in the United States of America

Library of Congress Cataloging-in-Publication Data

Ghosh, Arvin, 1937-
    Pricing and performance of initial public offerings in the United States / Arvin Ghosh.
        p. cm.
    Includes index.
    ISBN 0-7658-0326-7 (alk. paper)
    1. Going public (Securities)—United States. I. Title.

HG4028.S7G47   2006
332.63'222—dc22   2006040426

In the memory of my dear-departed
wife Kasturi ("Kay") Ghosh

Contents

List of Tables

Preface

Initial Public Offerings (IPOs) of securities are among the most significant phenomena in the United States stock markets in recent years. Before the 2000-2001 market downturn, hardly a week went by when more than a few companies did not become public, either in the organized stock exchanges or in the O-T-C market. In the technology-heavy Nasdaq (OTC) market, the role of the IPOs was crucial for its new vigor and growth where the Internet stocks supplied the key momentum. In the so-called "New Economy" in the 1990s, it was the IPO that ushered in the information technology revolution of the world.

In this research monograph, we have examined the pricing and the financial performance of the IPOs in the United States during 1990-2001. In chapter1, the rise and fall of the IPOs in the last decade is discussed. In chapter 2, the IPO process is delineated, from the start of the prospectus to the end of the "quiet period" and the aftermarket stabilization. In chapter 3, the mispricing and flipping of the *Internet* IPOs is analyzed. In chapter 4, the pricing and operating efficiency of the Nasdaq IPOs is delved into. In chapter 5, the pricing and long-run performance of the IPOs both in the New York Stock Exchange and in the Nasdaq markets is analyzed. Chapters 6 and 7 dealt with the pricing and performance of the venture-backed and nonventure-backed IPOs generally, and the *Internet* IPOs particularly, in respective chapters. In chapter 8 the role of underwriters as market makers is discussed. And in chapter 9, the accuracy of analysts' IPO earnings forecasts is discussed.

Chapter 10 summarizes the principal findings of the study and the recent revival of the IPO market and its place in capital formation. The latest developments in the realm of the United States IPOs is also discussed. The study, thus, brings forth the nature and consequences of the IPO phenomenon that had shaped our economy in the most significant way during the last decade.

1

Introduction
The IPO Phenomenon in the 1990s

Initial Public Offerings (IPOs) were the most prevalent form of security issues by firms wanting to raise capital in the United States during 1990-2000. The IPO phenomenon got a tremendous boost in the late 1990s by the popularity of Internet stocks. When Yahoo!, an online search engine, went public in March 1996, the investing public went agog with excitement, particularly the online traders, a new breed of individual investors. In the so-called 'bubble period' of 1998-1999, hardly a week went by when one or two IPOs, particularly Internet IPOs, did not appear in the capital market. In 1998, five IPOs had over 200 percent first-day returns, while in 1999, forty-eight IPOs had that distinction, with eight having returns of more than 400 percent on the first day. Also in 1999, 117 IPOs doubled their prices on the first day trading alone. It was quite possible that without the IPOs, the stock market boom of the 1990s would not have been sustained for such a long time and with such vigor as to push U.S. stock prices to historical highs. In the bull market of 1990s, it was the IPOs that created the climate of 'irrational exuberance,' particularly in the technology-heavy NASDAQ market.[1]

From its humble beginning in 1884 when Eastman Kodak went public with fourteen shareholders, the IPO market exploded during the last decade of the twentieth century when more than 4000 IPOs were issued in the United States and traded on organized exchanges and the over-the-counter market. Tens of millions of dollars were raised every month by companies offering stock to the public for the first time. According to Professor Jay Ritter, in the 1980s the average price of IPOs increased from the offer price to the first-day closing price by only 7 percent. However, the average first-day return tripled to 21 percent in the 1990s.[2] In the 1990s, institutional and individual investors alike were mesmerized by the huge profit potential in the IPO market. In the 1990s, the IPO market was "like the opening of the American West over 150 years ago—the transcontinental railroad, the Gold Rush and the availability of land made the opportunities seem limitless," to quote Linda Killian, et al., from their popular book, *IPOs for Everyone*.[3]

Unfortunately, with the stock market taking a sharp downturn after March 2000, many of these firms have succumbed to the market pressure and have gone out of business. But many well-established companies in the United States also entered the IPO market, most are still in business and a number of them are, in fact, thriving. Although the NASDAQ stock market had the largest number of IPO listings, the New York Stock Exchange (NYSE) also listed a significant number of IPOs. By studying the IPOs in these two markets, will we be able to understand the dynamics of the stock markets that shaped and molded the United States economy in the most fundamental way.

The IPOs During 1990-1995

The IPOs did not burst onto the scene, of course, in 1990. They had a long and checkered history before evolving into an effective tool for raising capital for companies wanting to go public. In their extensive database of 4,753 IPOs during 1970-1990, Professors Loughran and Ritter listed 876 IPOs during 1970-72, 634 IPOs during 1980-1982, and 1,315 IPOs during 1983-1985 in the United States alone.[4] Even before 1970, there were quite a few IPOs in the United States, as Linda Killian, et al., mentioned in their book. When we examine the data base maintained by the Securities Data Company (SDC), now owned by Thomson Financial, we find that during 1970-1972, the IPO market was quite strong, with an average of slightly over 300 IPOs per year, with an average offer price of about $9, and raising an average of over $3 million per issuance. But with the onset of the recessionary period in 1973, the IPO numbers started to dwindle. In the worst "stagflation" years of 1974-1975, IPOs were less than double digit in number, although the average offer price during 1973-1975 was higher than during the previous period. Nevertheless, the IPO market was up again after 1978 when the average number of IPOs per year was 378 during 1978-1985, the average offer price was $7, and the average amount of money raised was $9.59 million per issuance.[5]

The IPO business, however, had picked up in 1986-1987 before the stock market crash of 1987, when a record 533 IPO issues raised $24 billion in capital. Even in 1988, 255 IPOs raised $22.4 billion for the issuing firms. But 1989 was the slowest year in the six-year period (1983-1989) when 245 IPOs came into market raising $19.2 billion, down 55 percent from the peak in 1986. Also, new offerings from closed-end funds were scarcer in 1989. For the first time in those years, these investment companies that were listed on stock exchanges or the O-T-C market, did not have a dominant part in the IPO market. These funds issued only about $7 billion worth of new shares or slightly more than 50 percent of the total IPO volume. In the past, closed-end fund IPOs had accounted for 75 percent or more of the total capital raised.

The initial public offerings market fared even worse in 1990, mainly because of Iraq's occupation of Kuwait in August of that year and the impending threat of the Gulf War to be launched by the United States. Dollar volume of IPOs in 1990 slumped from 1989's already paltry level, to $10.2 billion. In 1990's fourth quarter, just fifty-nine IPOs were issued—the lowest quarterly total in more than ten years. And the $3 billion raised in the fourth quarter was the lowest in six years. The White House admitted that the United States economy was in recession, and predicted that the downturn would last until the coming summer. But the stock market ended its worst year since 1981, when the DJIA climbed to 2,633 on December 31, 1990. After a slow start in January 1991 with four deals, there were seven in February, eighteen in March, and twenty-eight in April. From then on the IPO market did not slow down again until September 1998. As a matter of fact, investment bankers sold $16.4 billion in shares from 360 IPOs, just behind the 1986 record of $18.3 billion. An additional 454 already-public companies sold over $29 billion more in new shares, making 1991 a record year for seasoned equity offerings, according to IDD Information Services, Inc. Leverage buyouts, which were the craze in the 1980s, almost died out as the 1990s dawned.

But 1992 turned out to be a banner year for the IPO market, as 595 were issued and $39.4 billion were raised from investors. The number soared to 170 in the first quarter, and after a summer slump, rebounded in the fourth quarter with 159 offerings. Biotechnology stocks dominated the new-issue market during the early part of the year, and finished strongly with technology-related issues. Fueling the IPO boom in that year was a bull market in small stocks, and as a result, the NASDAQ composite index rose to 676.95, closing the year with a 15.5 percent gain. Among the IPOs, Lone Star Steakhouse was a big winner with a 457 percent increase over its offer price, followed by Casino Magic with a 360 percent rise from its offer price by the end of the year. Starbucks went public in June of that year, with an offer price of $21.50 and finishing at $37 at the end of 1992.

Nineteen ninety three was also a very good year for the IPO stocks. More than 800 companies came to the equity market for the first time, with the volume totaling $57 billion, higher than the 1990's record of $40 billion. The IPOs' gain averaged 21 percent for the year. The biggest IPO issue that year was from a foreign company—a $2.7 billion offering of YPF Sociedad Anonima, Argentine's state-owned oil company. Next came a $2.1 billion offering from Allstate Corporation. Two trends were established in the underwriting business in that year: first, stock was preferred over bonds as a capital-raising vehicle, and second, strong IPO offerings came from Latin America, the Far East and Europe and listed in the United States stock markets. In 1994, the stock market had a lackluster performance when the Dow Jones Industrial Average (DJIA) rose by 2.14 percent to 3834.44, the NASDAQ lost 3.14 percent to 751.96, and the Russell 2000, the small-capitalization stock index, also lost 3.18 percent in that year. The largest IPO issuer in that year was TeleDenmark ($2,975 million) with an annual gain of 8.4 percent, but the second largest issuer—Istituto Nazionale Assicun, with a $2,866.6 million offering lost 15.6 percent for the whole year. OfficeMax gained 39.5 percent—the highest gain in that year among the IPOs, while Playtex Products lost 45.2 percent—the largest loss among the IPOs in that year.

In 1995, the fourth quarter was the strongest for the IPO market, with technology companies being hot that year. Internet companies supplying tools and applications for managing the World Wide Web started to appear for the first time. Open.Text, that provided search software for LANs, WANs and the Internet, went public with 3.6 million shares. Branded consumer names such as Gucci, Estee Lauder and Oakley launched successful IPOs, with Gucci up by 76 percent, Estee Lauder up by 34 percent, and Oakley gained 48 percent in share price by the end of that year. The IPO after-market was strong and showed no sign of weakening. Companies selling everything from jeans to bagels to flowers went public.

The IPOs in 1996-1999

The year 1996 was a watershed year for the United States IPOs. In February through early June of that year, there was a buying frenzy by institutions and individuals alike for any kind of high-technology or Internet IPOs, irrespective of their profit potentials—a forerunner of the event we witnessed again in 1999. Awash with 401 (K) funds, fund managers of the aggressive-growth mutual funds and microcap funds were the biggest buyers of IPOs. There were many IPOs whose first-day gains were over 50 percent of the offer price. Then came the summer when the IPO market cooled off considerably with many of the stocks losing more than 30 percent of their value. The last quarter of the year saw a new spurt in the IPO market that continued beyond 1996. In all, 872 IPOs were issued in that year raising $49.9 billion—the most ever from the IPO market. Business software, mortgage finance and telecommunications services were the strongest sectors in that year. Also, during the two years of 1995-1996, the average IPO gained nearly 30 percent on its first day of issuance—a remarkable feat indeed.

Even with their high initial prices, IPOs on average turned up below-market returns of 12.1 percent in 1996. This was much below 1995's average return of 33.9 percent and below 1996's DJIA return of 26 percent. In Table 1 we have provided the top ten and worst ten IPO performers for 1996. Here we find that Cyner Corp had an annual gain of 406 percent, followed by Outdoor Systems with an annual return of 321 percent. The worst performance was that of Cable & Co. Worldwide, with a negative annual return of 85 percent, followed by N-Vision Company, with a negative 83 percent annual return. The biggest story that year was the spin-off of AT&T Corporation's telecommunication units named Lucent Technologies, Inc. That year Yahoo went public in April at a $13 offer price and quickly shot up to $30, despite its question of future profitability. It was also the year of the largest foreign IPO issuance in the United States when Goldman, Sachs & Co. brought Deutsche Telecom AG, the German telecommunications company into the public domain.

Nineteen ninety-seven also was a very good year for the IPO market, but not as robust as 1996 because of a small downturn in October 1997 ("The October Effect"). In 1997, 629 IPOs raised over $39 billion, according to CommScan, Inc., a New York securities research company.[6] The year's offering, on average, returned just over 19

Table 1.1
Top 10 and Worst 10 Performance of the IPOs in 1996

Company	Offering Price	12/31/96 Price	% Change
A. The Best Performers			
Cymer	$9.50	$48.13	+406.6 %
Outdoor Systems	6.67	28.13	+321.9
Sipex	9.50	32.25	+239.5
Whittman-Hart	8.00	25.63	+220.3
Seibel Systems	8.50	27.00	+217.7
Paravant Computer Systems	1.67	5.25	+215.0
Sykes Enterprises	12.00	37.50	+212.5
Pride Automotive Group	5.00	15.38	+207.5
Sawtek	13.00	39.63	+204.8
Pacific Gateway Exchange	12.00	36.50	+204.2
B. The Worst Performers			
Cable & Co. Worldwide	$6.00	$0.88	-85.42%
N-Vision	5.00	0.81	-83.75
Kaye Kolts Associates	5.00	0.94	-81.25
Thermo-Mizer Environmental	5.00	0.94	-81.25
Riscorp	19.00	3.63	-80.92
Dignity Partners	12.00	2.63	-78.12
Pioneer Commercial Funding	5.00	1.25	-75.00
Multicom Publishing	6.50	1.63	-75.00
Applewoods	2.50	0.63	-75.00
Infonautics	14.00	3.75	-73.21

Source: Securities Data Co./ Thomson Financial

percent, calculated annually, as compared with the DJIA of 22.6 percent, and 20.5 percent for the small stock Russell 2000 index. Those who bought after the first day gained on average of 7.2 percent annual return. The biggest deals that year were the $438 million offering of car rental company Hertz Corp., the $611 million offering of Polo Ralph Lauren, and the $798 million offering of the oil drilling company Santa Fe International, a unit of Kuwait Petroleum. Also debuting that year were the online book-selling company Amazon.com with an offer price of $18 a share which rose nearly 70 percent in first-day trading, and the semiconductor maker

Rambus which was offered at $12 a share and doubled in price at the end of first-day trading.

But 1998 was a lackluster year for the IPO market. There were only 373 IPOs that came to the market, down about 40 percent in number from 1997. In terms of total dollar volume, newly-issued companies raised slightly more than $36.5 billion, down 10 percent from the 1997 total, and down 29 percent from the 1996 total. Also, IPOs rose on average by less than 9 percent from their opening prices, while the S & P 500 stock index rose by 31 percent. But some of the biggest IPOs took place that year when Du Pont Co. sold its subsidiary Conoco, Inc. in the IPO market. Investors paid $44 billion for that company. They also paid $5.6 billion for the Swiss telecom concern Swisscom AG, and $18 billion for the offering of NTT Mobile Communications Network, Inc., a former subsidiary of the Japanese mobile telecommunications company NTT DoCoMo. Also in that year online auctioneer eBay Inc. went public, surging sixteen-fold from its September offering price of $18 to a high of $301. At its peak, eBay had the same market capitalization of Federated Department Stores, Inc., and half the market value of Sears, Roebuck & Co., the venerated department store chain in America.

The year 1999 was *The Year of the IPOs*, particularly for Internet IPOs. The surge in the IPO market witnessed in late 1998 carried through all of 1999 and dried up only in March 2000 when the stock market in general, and the IPO market in particular, went sour. Newly-issued public companies in that year were 544 in number, up from 373 in 1998, but less than the record set in 1996 of 872 companies coming to the public stock markets for the first time. The IPOs in 1999 raised $69.1 billion, which was nearly double the 1998 total of $36.5 billion, and close to 40 percent higher than the previous record of $49.9 billion in 1996, according to the Securities Data Company of Thomson Financial. These numbers included both large and small capitalization companies, but excluded closed-end mutual funds and real estate investment trusts. As of June 1999, IPOs soared an average 43 percent from their opening price, compared to 8.5 percent gain of the S&P 500 stock index.

Many large and small companies went public that year, with Web-based and technology start-ups being the most prominent. The biggest IPO in the U.S. history occurred that year when UPS, in early November, raised $4.38 billion. Goldman, Sachs & Co. raised $2.72

billion in the U.S. when it went public in May for the first time. But price-performance-wise, it was the software company VA Software Systems, Inc. which ruled the roost when its shares soared 697.50 percent on the first day of trading on December 9, heading the list of all-time first-day IPO price increases. MarketWatch.Com Inc. jumped 474 percent in its first day trading in January, and iVillage Inc. soared 232 percent on its first-day debut in March of that year. IPOs such as Juniper Networks and Gadzoox Networks, which made their debut in June and July, rose 191 percent and 256 percent, respectively, on their first day of trading. Business-to-business IPO, FreeMarkets, Inc. rose 483 percent on its first-day trading in December 1999. According to the World Finance Net.Com, 117 or 23 percent of the year's IPOs had increased more than 100 percent in price on the first day of trading. As a matter of fact, all but one (theglobe.com being offered in public in November 1998 was the exception) of the twenty-five best first-day IPO performances took place in 1999.

In Table 2, we have given the annual price-performance statistics of the top ten United States IPOs by December 31, 1999. Here we find that the top performer was an investment holding company called Internet Capital Group, with an incredible 5,567 percent increase in share price from the offer price during only five months. Next came Commerce One, another e-commerce company with a stock price increase of 2,707.1 percent for the whole year. All of the other eight companies were either Internet companies, or software equipment or management companies like Brocade Comm.Systems and Vignett, respectively.

But not all IPOs performed well in 1999. Table 2 also shows ten worst performances by IPO firms during 1999. Here Value America topped the list, with a drop of 78 percent through December 31, from its offer price of $23.00, although its first-day price gain of share was 140 percent. Next came Insurance Management Solutions with a price decline of 77.3 percent from its offer price of $11. Interestingly, almost all the companies in the ten worst performance list were in the finance or manufacturing sectors, not in the Internet-related businesses. Also some IPOs, like Vitaninshoppe.com (VSHP), 1-800-flowers.com (FLWS), and Mothernature.com (MTHR) fell in price during the first day of trading. The last two companies have lost considerable market capitalization since going public.

Table 1.2
Top 10 and Worst 10 Annualized Performances of the IPOs in 1999

Company	Offer Price	% Change from Offer Price	
		First Day's Trading	December 31
A. The Best Performers			
Internet Capital Group (ICGE)	$12.00	+103.7 %	+5,567.0 %
Commerce One (CMRC)	21.00	+190.3	+2,707.1
Purchasepro.com (PPRO)	12.00	+117.7	+2,479.7
VerticalNet (VERT)	16.00	+183.6	+1,950.0
Brocade Comm. Systems (BRCD)	19.00	+138.2	+1,763.2
Vignette (VIGN)	19.00	+124.7	+1,615.8
Liberate Technologies (LBRT)	16.00	+26.6	+1,506.3
Redback Networks (RBAK)	23.00	+296.6	+1,443.5
Ariba (ARBA)	23.00	+291.3	+1,442.4
Red Hat (RHAT)	14.00	+271.4	+1,408.9
B. The Worst Performers			
Value America (VUSA)	$23.00	+140.0%	-78.0%
Insurance Mgmt Solutions (INMG)	11.00	Unch.	-77.3
Stalia Terminals (STNV)	20.00	-8.1	-73.1
Trion Technology (TRIN)	7.00	+22.3	-69.6
Argosy Education (ARGY)	14.00	-4.0	-68.3
Fashionmall.com (FASH)	13.00	Unch.	-65.4
Skechers USA (SKX)	11.00	-3.4	-65.4
FlashNet Communications (FLAS)	17.00	+156.6	-63.6
HI-Q Wason (HIQW)	7.00	-4.4	-62.4
Packaged Ice (ICED)	8.50	-2.9	-61.8

Source: Securities Data Company/Thomson Financial.

The Internet Bubble

It was the Internet stocks that fueled the IPO outburst in the late 1990s. In 1991 the World Wide Web (WWW) was born when the new HTML code let programmers combine words, pictures and sound on web pages. When in 1993, Marc Andreesen and fellow University of Illinois students developed *Mossaic* to browse the Web effectively, the number of users grew by 341,000 percent by year's end. Within a very short time, Web-based Internet browsing came into being and Online business was launched. It was online trading, in turn, that helped give rise to the volatile first-day and after-market performances for Internet IPOs. And the significance of the Internet in reshaping both the United States and the world economy was enormous. It has changed such businesses as the selling of airline tickets and the distribution of financial service products. It ushered in the information technology we know today.

The Internet stocks took off when the first Web browser Netscape Communications (NSCP) came into being in 1995. It went public on August 1 of that year and its share prices soared 108 percent on its first day. In 1996, Yahoo went public, and the stock market value of the company was nearly $1 billion within a year. Then in 1997, the first e-commerce company Amazon.com went public. In 1998, during its first half, demand for IPO stocks was so robust that on average forty-four new issues a month were floated. But in August, the IPO market fell to nineteen issues due to the Russian debt default. It sank to only three issues in September and five in November. Since then, the Internet stocks have dominated the IPO market. For example, eBay's stock skyrocketed to a high of $234.16 in November 1998 from its opening level of $18 in September of that year. Ticketmaster Online.City Search (TMCS) went up 243 percent from its offering price of $14 to open at $48 per share on its first day in 1998. In the last two months of 1998, two-thirds of Internet IPOs increased in value by 100 percent or more in the first day of trading. Nine out of the top ten performing IPOs that year were Internet stocks. The frenzy surrounding Internet stocks had drastically distorted some companies' price-earning ratios. At one point eBay, the Internet auction site, was trading at 10,000 times its earnings! Its earnings were a measly two cents per share, but it was carrying a stock price of $200-plus per share at that time.

Thus 1999 became the banner year for Internet IPOs when 240 Internet companies went public and Dow Jones Internet index went up by 167 percent for the year. Internet IPOs that year raised more than $69 billion, 39 percent more than in 1996, the second-biggest year for the IPOs. In 1999, some of the IPO's first-day gains were astonishing, to say the least. VA Software Corp.(LNUX) jumped a record 733 percent in first-day trading in early December of 1999. Internet IPOs such as theglobe.com soared from an initial offering price of $9 per share to more than $63 on its first day—up more than 600 percent. Red Hat (RHAT), a Linux distributor, rose 272 percent on its first day of trading in August of that year.

Yahoo's market capitalization became $34 billion in that year. iVillage, which ran several women's and family websites, had revenues of $6 million in the first quarter and expenses of $24 million, when it went public in March 1999. But its stock price was up 233 percent on the first day, and its market value became $1.6 billion. By June 1999, CMGI's stock price rose almost 400 times in five years; Yahoo was up about 80 times in three years; Amazon was up forty-five times in two years; and eBay was up twenty times in just eight months. Amazon's market capitalization rose to $25 billion which took Walmart twenty-seven years to reach. Both Amazon and AOL rose more than 6,000 percent in July 1999 since their IPO debuts.

Internet IPOs got a tremendous boost from the venture capitalists. Generally, a large number of IPOs are backed by venture capital firms. In 1998, venture capitalists put $13.7 billion into 2,023 start-ups, up from $2.5 billion invested in 627 companies in 1994. In 1999, Internet companies received nearly $20 billion in venture capital funding. As a matter of fact, hardly there was a successful Internet company in that year which did not receive funding from at least one big-name venture capitalist. Venture capital became the incubator that nurtured the Internet companies by providing money for start-up and later expansion—a process vital for growth in any sector of the economy.

Internet stocks also got strong 'buy' recommendations from many well-known financial analysts employed by large brokerage houses. Henry Blodget, a star Internet analyst at Merrill Lynch was so high on Internet stocks that he seemed to see only the profit potentials for all the stocks he recommended. Similarly, Jack Grubman at Citigroup's Smith Barney was bullish on all telecommunications stocks even when some of them went sour. Morgan Stanley's tech-stock analyst Mary Meeker was dubbed "queen of the Internet" for her continuous upbeat calls on many highflying tech stocks. All the favorable recommendations from these and other analysts had created such a bullish atmosphere for the Internet stocks that many of them gained tremendously in price, including on their first day of trading.

In Table 3, we have shown the highest first-day returns of twenty-five IPO stocks issued in 1999, along with the offer price and first-day opening and closing prices of these companies. We find that VA Software Corporation—an Internet company—had the incredible first-day return of almost 700 percent, followed by a 525 percent first-day return of Foundry Networks, Inc. Out of the other four IPOs with over 400 percent first-day returns, three were also Internet companies. There were six companies whose first-day returns were over

Table 1.3
Highest First-Day Gains of 25 IPOs, 1999

Company	Offer Price	First Day Opening Price	First Day Closing Price	First Day Return
1. Value Software Corp.	$30.00	$299.00	$239.25	+697.50
percent				
2. Foundry Networks, Inc.	25.00	109.00	156.25	+525.00
3. FreeMarkets, Inc.	48.00	248.00	280.00	+483.33
4. MarketWatch. Com	17.00	90.00	97.50	+473.53
5. Akamai Technologies, Inc.	26.00	110.00	145.19	+458.42
6. Blue Coat Systems, Inc.	24.00	110.00	126.38	+426.58
7. Sycamore Networks, Inc.	38.00	270.00	184.75	+386.18
8. Ask Jeeves, Inc.	14.00	72.00	64.94	+363.86
9. Finisar Corporation	19.00	95.00	86,88	+357.26
10. Crossroads Systems, Inc.	18.00	36.50	78.72	+337.33
11. Priceline.com Inc.	16.00	81.00	69.00	+331.25
12. Wireless Facilities, Inc.	15.00	37.50	62.00	+313.33
13. WebMD Corp.	8.00	21.88	31.38	+292.25
14. Ariba, Inc.	23.00	61.00	90.00	+291.30
15. Experdia, Inc.	14.00	37.00	53.44	+291.71
16. Red Hat, Inc.	14.00	46.00	52.06	+271.86
17. Digital Impact, Inc.	15.00	34.00	55.50	+270.00
18. Redback Networks, Inc.	23.00	67.25	84.13	+265.78
19. KANA Software, Inc.	15.00	50.50	51.50	+243.33
20. Quest Software, Inc.	14.00	20.50	47.00	+235.71
21. Chinadotcom Corp.	20.00	45.75	67.11	+235.55
22. iVillage, Inc.	24.00	95.88	80.13	+233.88
23. Paradyne Networks, Inc.	17.00	50.00	56.25	+230.88
24. Copper Mountain Networks	21.00	63.00	68.44	+225.90
25. Extreme Networks, Inc.	17.00	54.00	55.38	+225.76

Source: Hoover.com, 1999.

300 percent, followed by fourteen companies with first-day gains over 200 percent. *As a matter of fact, there were no IPOs in this list whose first-day return was not 200 percent or more.* In all, in this table of twenty-five companies, twenty-one, or almost 85 percent, were *Internet-related* companies.

Some Internet companies grew such large market capitalizations that they equalled or surpassed some of the well-established *Fortune 500* companies. Table 4 shows this comparison in 1999. Here we find that America Online's market capitalization was almost equal to Pfizer's, which started in the nineteenth century and was number fifty-three on *Fortune* magazine's list of 500 largest United States companies in 2000 in terms of revenues. Similarly, Yahoo's market capitalization was slightly lower than Allied Signal, a company be-

Table 1.4
Market Capitalization of 10 Largest Internet Companies
as Compared to Fortune's 100 Largest Companies, 1999

Internet Company	Market Capitalization	Fortune Company	Market Capitalization
America Online	$149.8 billion	Pfizer Corp.	$149.8 billion
Yahoo	34.5	Allied Signal	34.7
eBay	24.0	JP Morgan	24.3
Amazon.com	23.0	Alcoa Corp.	23.0
Priceline.com	17.9	FDX (FedEx)	17.7
@Home	16.8	Lockheed Martin	16.9
E*Trade	12.9	AMR (Amer. Airlines)	13.5
CMGI	11.2	Ingersoll Rand	11.4
Excite	8.4	Mattel	8.0
RealNetworks	5.7	Toys "R" Us	5.5

Source: Annual Report of the respective companies for 1999.

longing to the Dow Jones Industrial Average (DJIA) composed of thirty very large firms in the United States. Amazon.com was exactly equal to Alcoa, another DJIA company. E*Trade Group, Inc., which started in 1994 and went public in the summer of 1996, was bigger in market capitalization than AMR, a diversified company which was number 77 on *Fortune*'s list of 500 largest companies in the United States in 1999.

Some large Internet companies also grew by mergers and acquisitions of smaller Internet companies. Table 5 given the details of some notable acquisitions of this kind. We find that, although Home Network had the largest single merger in dollars, Yahoo had the largest total dollar volumes in that year. America Online, after acquiring Netscape Communications, became so big that it acquired the Time Warner Corp. in January 2000. When we add other deals by some of these companies, we find that Yahoo also took significant equity positions in Viaweb, Yoyodyne, and 411 dot.com companies. Similarly, America Online had deals with CompuServe, When.com, PersonaLogic, ImagiNation, Personal Library Software, Extreme Fans, and Mirabilis.[7] Although not in 1999, JDS Uniphase, bought E-Tek Dynamics, Inc. for $15 billion in January 2000, when its market capitalization was over $60 billion. It also bought Optical Coating Laboratory, Inc. for $2.8 billion in 2000.

The year 2000 started very auspiciously for the IPO companies. The IPO calendar was packed in January of that year. While the number of IPOs doubled from 1999s record-breaking first quarter,

Table 1.5
Mergers and Acquisitions Among Internet Stocks, 1999

Acquiring Company	Acquired Company	Amount in Dollars
Home Network	Excite	$6.7 billion
Yahoo	Broadcast.com	5.7 billion
Yahoo	GeoCities	4.6 billion
America Online	Netscape	4.2 billion
EBay	Butterfield & Butterfield	260 million
Amazon	Alexa Internet	250 million
Amazon	Exchane.com	200 million

Source: *Fortune* magazine, June 7, 1999

the total proceeds of the IPOs during the first quarter of 2000 nearly trippled to $32.1 billion, as a number of large issues were traded in public for the first time. IPOs such as Infineon Technologies (IFX) raised $5.2 billion and John Hancock Financial Services, Inc. (JHF) raised $1.7 billion in public offerings. In that first quarter of 2000, technology issues continued to lead the way. Business to business (B2B) software company Webmethods Inc (WEBM) posted that quarter's highest first-day gain of 508 percent, followed by Japanese e-mail service provider Crayfish Inc. which jumped 414 percent in its first day trading. There was quite a few international companies that joined in the IPO frenzy in the U.S. stock markets at that time.

But the IPO market, especially the Internet stocks, went sour after March 2000. NASDAQ was at its peak of 5,048.62 on March 10, and the DJIA previously was at its highest level on January 14, when it stood at 11,722.98. After that, the DJIA started to go downhill, just as the NASDAQ did after March 10. Even some of the IPOs which gained spectacularly in the first quarter, came tumbling down during the second quarter of 2000. For example, Palm Inc., the maker of handheld computer which went up to $165 during March, came down below its offer price of $38 during the first week of April 2000. By the end of 2000, the NASDAQ index fell by 51 percent, and the DJIA by almost 8 percent, from their historic highs.

It was soon apparent that the Internet sector was simply overextended where real new ideas for products or services became few and far between. At the same time, money poured in from all quarters—institutional and individual alike—including venture capitalists. But most of the Internet companies had little or no earnings, and would be in the red for the foreseeable future. As a result, the collapse of the Internet market was inevitable as the valuation of these stocks was simply too high. The question was when. And when the NASDAQ market did take a nosedive after March of 2000, it brought down the whole IPO market as well, including the Internet stocks. The total loss in the 'dot-com bubble' was put at $4 trillion, as reported in the Wall Street Journal.[8]

The Meltdown after March 2000

The year 2000 started as a strong market for IPO issuance when by February of that year, some thirty-one IPOs had already hit the market and fifteen of them had enjoyed a first-day price increase of double their offer prices. But after January 14 and March 10, 2000, when the DJIA and NASDAQ reached their highest points, respectively, and the stock market bubble was about to burst, the IPO market started to go down. Most of the sixty-seven IPOs brought to market before October 2001, were traded below their offering prices. And when the terrorist attack on the World Trade Center came on 9/11, that September of 2001 was the first month since December 1975 in which there were no IPOs, according to the SDC/ Thomson Financial. That company collected data for nineteen individual months with no IPO offerings since 1970, and eighteen of these nineteen occurred between July 1973 and December 1975—the worst recession the country faced after the World War II.

The 'dot-com bust' led to the IPO downturn in 2000 when prices of many IPOs fell so sharply as to become virtually worthless. In Table 6, we have shown the worst performance of thirty IPO stocks during 2001-2002 whose first-day returns were over 200 percent. When we compare this table with Table 3, we find that VA Software Corporation—the company with the highest first-day return—was also the company with the worst decline in this period. This company had a first-day offer price of $30 which shot up to $239.25 at the close of that trading day, but when we take the fifty-two-week low of $0.67 cents during 2001-2002, we see that its return had declined over 99.99 percent in the same period! Almost the same way, Akamai Technologies was the fifth highest in Table 1.3, but became the third worst company in performance in Table 6.

Most of the other companies that had the best performances in 1999 had also in Table 1.6's list of worst performances in 2001-2002, although not in the same order. For example, Redback Net-

Table 1.6
Poor Performance of 30 IPO Firms Where First-Day Returns
Were Over 200 Percent

Company	First-Day Closing Price	52-Week Low (2001-2002)	% Decline from First-Day Closing Price
VA Software Corp.	$239.25	$0.67	-99.99%
Redback Networks	84.13	0.24	-99.99
Akamai Technologies, Inc.	145.19	0.56	-99.99
Crossroads Systems, Inc.	126.38	0.38	-99.99
Finisar Corp.	86.88	0.42	-99.99
Tut Systems, Inc.	57.50	0.41	-99.00
KANA Software	51.50	0.59	-99.00
Sycamore Networks	184.75	2.20	-99.00
FreeMarkets, Inc.	280.00	3.50	-99.00
Ask Jeeves	64.94	0.92	-99.00
Ariba	90.00	1.30	-99.00
Extensity, Inc	71.25	1.11	-98.00
Paradyne Networks, Inc.	56.25	0.95	-98.00
Marimba	60.56	1.10	-98.00
Blue Coat Systems, Inc.	126.38	2.50	-98.00
WebMethods, Inc.	212.63	4.25	-98.00
Turnstore Systems, Inc.	97.00	2.00	-98.00
Neoforma, Inc.	52.38	7.20	-86.00
Digital Impact	55.50	1.23	-98.00
IVillage	80.13	1.82	-98.00
Foundry Networks, Inc	156.25	4.08	-97.00
Chinadot Corp.	67.11	1.90	-97.00
TheStreet.com	60.00	1.91	-97.00
MarketWatch.com	97.50	3.88	-96.00
Extreme Networks, Inc.	55.38	2.33	-96.00
Copper Mountain Networks	68.44	3.17	-95.00
Red Hat	52.06	3.46	-93.00
Priceline.com	59.00	6.30	-89.00
Quest Software	47.00	7.30	-84.00
WebMD	31.38	4.25	-86.00

Source: Securities Data Company/Thomson Financial.

works was number two on the worst performance list in Table 6, but was number eighteen on the best performance list of Table 3. The least worst performance in Table 6 was that of Quest Software Corp. whose decline from its first-day closing price was 84 percent, while it was number 13 in Table 3, with the first-day return over 292 percent.

In 2002, the number of IPOs in the U.S. stock markets hit a two-decade low of just 83 deals, raising $22.6 billion, the lowest since the early 1990s. The first IPO of 2002 was a stock named Carolina Group that was the Lorrillard tobacco operations of Loews Corporation. It was a tracking stock that confers on shareholders a chance to obtain the economic benefits of a business, but generally limits the ownership and voting rights of these shareholders. The conflict of interest comes mostly in voting rights where the tracking stocks carry with them less voting power, with the parent company's shareholders having almost complete control of all aspects of the unit's business. As a result, short of allowing investors a chance to separate out the economic potential, there are few other benefits for investors. That is why tracking stocks are not very common. There were none in 2001, with the last one coming from Alcatel Optronics, a business unit of France's Alcatel SA, back in October of 2000. It was sold at $71.95 on the opening day, but had lost more than 90 percent of its value by the end of January 2002.

Two thousand two was also the year when the web-based online companies became few in number. Only the well-established parent companies with proven record of profitability spun off their subsidiaries as IPOs. Technology companies, which accounted for 70 percent of public offerings in the overheated stock markets between 1997 and 1999, comprised less than one-third in the first quarter of 2002. In that year leverage buyout firms and large companies spinning off subsidiaries were the main sources of new stock offerings. In 1999, the median age of companies with new stock offerings was four years only. In 2002, it was more than fifteen years. According to Professor Jay Ritter, 58 percent of the companies that completed new stock offerings in 2002 were profitable, compared with 18.8 percent in 2000.[9]

Also, more IPO companies listed on the NYSE rather than the NASDAQ in 2002. By the first week of May 2002, the NYSE, and not the NASDAQ stock market, had sixteen of the twenty-four major underwritten initial public offerings (IPOs). For the technology companies the stricter rules of the NYSE were a hindrance, while more mature companies in fairly stable businesses and at or near profitability were more attracted to the NYSE. In the late 1990s, some analysts even suggested that the NYSE was out of touch by not giving Internet and technological companies any opportunity to list there.

But the NYSE had already made two changes within the past few years to its listing requirements that had helped them in 2001 and

2002—the lean years for the IPO market. First, it created a "market cap/revenue" rule that allowed companies with global market capitalization of $1 billion and annual revenue of $100 million to list, by getting around previous more stringent requirements for cash flows and profits. Secondly, the NYSE has also created an "affiliate standard," allowing units of companies that were listed on the exchange, to list there as well, even if they did not otherwise meet the standards. Here many of the largest domestic IPOs in history have come from unit curve outs ("tracking stocks"), offerings from AT&T, Kraft Foods Inc., and Travelers Property & Casualty Corp.—all on the NYSE.

The summer of 2002, however, saw little surge in IPO issuance. More than seventy companies were lined up to go public. That number was much smaller than 366 that were in the pipeline in 2000, but more than at the same time in 2001 when fifty-six companies were waiting. Only the Web-based companies became successful, such as Overstock.com Inc., an online retailer that sold three million shares at between $12 and $16 a share. Two other Web-based offerings that year gained in share prices. Online-payment company Paypal Inc. went public on February 15, 2002, and rose 55 percent on its first day. JetBlue Airways Corp. was the best gainer of that year, soaring 67 percent on the first day on April 12, 2002, to $45 a share from its initial $27, because of strong earnings and revenues. In May of 2002, the DVD-rental service company Netflix Inc. sold 5.5 million shares at $15 each, and gained 12 percent on its first day.

IPO issuance became so rare that in January 2003, not a single IPO was offered, which had not happened since 1974. The weakened U.S. economy and the talk of impending war with Iraq surely derailed the IPO offerings. We have to recall that the financial crisis of the world in September of 1998 slowed down the IPO offer; but when the crisis subsided, IPO offerings came roaring back soon after that which became the most successful period in the IPO history. Generally, the investment bankers and underwriters arrange the "roadshows" for the impending investors where the executives of the prospective IPO companies would be present. But that did not occur in January 2003. The last successful IPO that took place was on December 12, 2002, when the natural gas company Crosstex Energy L.P. raised $40 million through A. G. Edwards & Sons, with an offer price of $20. After that, it was price cuts, delays and first-day losses, for the two IPOs—Accredited Home Lenders Holding

Co. and Infinity Property & casualty Corp—issued in February 2003. There were just twenty-one public offerings by the end of September 2003 as compared to 406 back in 2000.

That the IPO market has turned from the seller's market in the 1990s to the institutional buyers' market in 2002-2003, can be seen by the fact that the latter group had determined the price mainly, not an unrealistically high offer price of yesteryears. The number of deals that were priced below their intended range—typically a $2 "window" that underwriters set in filing registration statements with the SEC—reached a record high in 2002, according to SDO/Thomson Financial. The drying up phenomenon of the IPO market in recent years can be found in the comment made by Mr. David Weild, Vice Chairman of NASDAQ: "This is a long walk in the desert."[10] The result is that we may not see the kind of "irrational exuberance" as we witnessed in the late 1990s, for the foreseeable future in the United States.

Notes

1. "Irrational Exuberance" was first uttered by the Federal Reserve Board Chairman Alan Greenspan in a speech on December 5, 1996.
2. See Jay Ritter's *Foreward* in Linda Killian, Kathleen Smith and William Smith's *IPOs for Everyone*, 2001.
3. *IPOs for Everyone*, Appendix C.
4. For the list of the IPOs issued during this period, see Tim Loughran and Jay Ritter's article "The New Issues Puzzle," in the *Journal of Finance*, March 1995.
5. For almost all the calculations, we have used Securities Data Company (SDO)/ Thomson Financial data base as our main source of IPO data gatherings.
6. CommScan, Inc.'s report was published in the *Wall Street Journal*, Jan. 2, 1998.
7. See *Fortune* magazine, June 7, 1999, p. 68.
8. *The Wall Street Journal*, February 12, 2002, p. A 21.
9. Jay Ritter, quoted in his web site.
10. Quoted in the *Wall Street Journal*, April 29, 2002.

References

Doffou, A., 2002, "Testing for Bubbles in the Internet Stock Market," *Working Paper*, September, 1-9.

Fox, J., 1999, "Net Stock Rules: Masters of a Parallel Universe," *Fortune*, June 7, 66-72.

Killian, L, K. Smith, and W. Smith, *IPOs for Everyone*, John Wiley & Sons, 2001.

Lee, J., 2000, "Internet Nosedive," *Money*, April, 11-15.

Loughran, T. and J. R. Ritter, 1995, "The New Issues Puzzle," *Journal of Finance* 50, 23-51.

Saunders, A., 2000, "Why Are So Many New Stock Issues Underpriced?" *Financial Markets*, Section II, 119-128.

Shiller, R.J., 2001, *Irrational Exuberance*, New York: Broadway Books, (paper).

The Wall Street Journal, Year-end Review Issues, covering 1990-2002.

2

The IPO Process

Initial Public Offerings (IPOs) are the first time that a company sells stock to the public. An IPO is a type of a primary offering, which occurs whenever a company sells new securities, and differs from a secondary offering, which is the public sale of previously issued securities, usually held by insiders. A company that is thinking of going public should start acting like a public company as much as two years in advance of the IPO. Several steps should be taken at that time, include preparing detailed financial statements on a regular basis and developing a business plan.

An IPO must be timed correctly if it is to be successful. Some rules of thumb for a company considering an IPO are that the company is growing, that it has a definite need for much larger funding, that it has a "good story," and that it is a good time in the market for this type of company.[1] Poor timing will result in little interest and few sales. For example, immediately after the 1987 crash of the stock market, almost all pending IPO deals were cancelled because the investors were leery of the market. Consequently, IPOs were not seen as the sure thing needed to get newly impoverished firms back into solvency.

Once a company decides to go public, it needs to select an IPO team, consisting of the lead investment bank, a public accountant, and a law firm. The IPO process officially begins with what is typically called an "all-hands" meeting. At that meeting, which usually takes place six to eight weeks before a company officially registers with the Securities and Exchange Commission (SEC), all the members of the IPO team plan a time line for going public and assign certain duties to each member.

Preparation of the Prospectus

The most important and time-consuming task facing the IPO team is the development of the *prospectus*, a document that basically serves as a brochure for the company. The Securities Act of 1933 mandates that the company and its counsel draft a registration statement for filing with the SEC, the purpose of the registration and disclosure requirements are to underscore the fact that the public has proper and reliable information about the securities that are going to be sold. Once the registration statement is filed with the SEC, it is transformed into the preliminary prospectus or "Red Herring" (so-called because of the red band of legal terms running vertically on the left hand side of the cover of the prospectus). It is the most important document used to market the IPO to the prospective investors.

The prospectus includes financial data for a company extending over the past five years, if applicable, information on the management team, and a descriptive of a company's target market, competitors, and growth strategy. There is a lot of other important information in the prospectus and the underwriting team goes to great lengths to make sure that it is accurate. Since the SEC imposes a "quiet period" on companies once they file for an IPO which generally lasts until twenty-five days after the stock starts public trading, the prospectus will have to do most of the talking and selling for the management team.

An analysis of initial public offerings indicates that the IPO process constitutes five distinct phases: (i) preparation of the IPO prospectus and submission to the SEC for approval; (ii) selecting the lead underwriter to form the syndicate and sell the stock to the public; (iii) organizing the "road show" to present the IPO's appeals and prospects to the investors, mainly the institutional investors; (iv) setting the offer price and the number of shares to be offered to the public, either through the organized exchanges or through the over-the-counter market; (v) and finally, developing the aftermarket position, after observing the 'quiet period.' The IPO will be more successful, the more these five steps are executed smoothly. Much more important is creating a 'buzz' among the investing public about the IPO, mainly through the media and the analysts' recommendation of the large brokerage houses.

Role of the Underwriters

One of the most crucial tasks of the IPO firm is to select the lead underwriter that is generally an investment bank. Selection of the underwriter depends on the investment banker's reputation, expertise and quality of research in the industry where the IPO competes. The lead underwriter becomes the book- running manager who forms the syndicate and becomes in charge of the whole IPO process. The initial agreement between the underwriter and the issuing company is called the *letter of intent* that protects the underwriter against any uncovered expenses in the event that the offer is withdrawn. It also specifies the gross spread (usually 7 percent) of the underwriter and a commitment of the company to grant a 15 percent overallotment option to the underwriter. The letter of intent remains valid until the underwriting agreement is executed at the time of pricing the shares.

After completing the due-diligence process, the co-managers, executives of the company, and their buyers prepare the form S-1 registration statement. In the S-1, the company offers extensive disclosures and descriptions of its business, history, risk, management, common stock and performance, as prescribed by the regulations for the issuance of securities under the Securities Act of 1933. The issuer also includes a preliminary filing range for the expected price of the IPO in the S-1 form. The S-1 also contains a copy of the preliminary prospectus to be used in the offering. The company files the S-1 with the SEC, establishing the "registration date" and the starting of the official registration process.

While the filing with the SEC is done and prospectus is prepared and filed with the SEC, the lead underwriter must then assemble a syndicate of other investment banks that will sell the deal. Each bank in the syndicate will get a certain number of shares in the IPO to sell to its clients. The syndicate then gathers indications of interest to see what kind of initial demand there is for the deal. Syndicates usually include investment banks that have complementary client bases, such as those based in certain regions of the country and/or an international clientele. We have to understand that the underwriters are the ones who provide certification, marketing and monitoring services to the IPO issuers. The underwriters risk their reputation with every IPO they underwrite and have to ensure the investors that the issuing company has fairly and accurately represented itself. Investors will count of the underwriters' due diligence as a sign of trust in the quality of the issuer.

As mentioned before, the underwriters generally receive a 7 percent spread. As the majority of the finance literature indicates, only a small percentage of underwriters ever agreed to a fee below 7 percent. Similarly, a spread above 7 percent is also very rare. Professor Hsuan-chi Chen and Jay Ritter have studied the underwriters' spread for 1,111 IPOs raising between $20 million and $80 million in the United States during 1995-1998, and found that more than 90 percent of issuers paid gross spreads of exactly 7 percent.[2] But it was not so in the previous decade. In the 1985-1987 period, only about a quarter of moderate size IPOs had a spread of exactly 7 percent. Chen and Ritter suggest that several features of the IPO underwriting market are conducive to spreads above competitive levels. Their study implies that the importance of analysts coverage, buy recommendations, and the underwriter's prestige, encourage for a high underwriter spread of 7 percent, not seen in other countries of the world.

The Road Show and Bookbuilding Process

Once the prospectus is ready and approved by the SEC, and the leading underwriter is selected, the company is ready to begin the "road show," i.e., presenting its case for the initial public offering to the investors, mainly the institutional investors around the country. Here the company officials make numerous presentations to the investors about the prospects of the company along with future profit potential. Generally, these road shows last three to four weeks and include two or more meetings per day with both retail sales people and institutional investors. The typical U.S. stops on the road show include New York City, San Francisco, Boston, Chicago, and Los Angeles. If appropriate, international destinations like London, Tokyo or Hong Kong may also be included.

Presentations and public relations can make or break an IPO. How a company's management team performs on the road show is perhaps the most crucial factor determining the success of the "road show". Companies need to impress the institutional investors so that at least a few of them are willing to buy a significant stake in the company. Only institutional investors, retail sales people and wealthy people are invited to attend the road show meetings where a company's business prospects—discussed only minimally in a prospectus—are talked about quite openly. According to the Securities and Exchange Commission, such discussions are legal, as long as they are done orally. However, the SEC has proposed new rules that, if approved, will make it easier for companies to broadcast their road shows over the Internet.

Once the road show ends and the final prospectus is printed and distributed to the investors, the company management meet with their lead underwriter to choose the final offer price and the size of the offering. However, the underwriter is in no position to sell shares to the public before the effective date of going public by the company. By gauging the feelings of the prospective investors throughout the country, the underwriter tries to suggest an appropriate price range based on expected demand for the deal and other market conditions.

The lead underwriter, also known as the "book manager" or "book runner," gathers and controls the information concerning the potential orders from all the other underwriters. The book manager consolidates this information into a "book" that is used to gauge demand at different prices and then to price the issue within the proper range. Thus book-building consists of three main steps. The first step is that the book manager has to determine which investors will be invited to participate. Generally, the small retail investors are not included in book-building efforts, although they may be allocated a small percentage of shares at the price to be fixed later. The second step is that the prospective investors are asked to submit their indications of interest. The investors may submit a *strike bid* which means that the bidder is preferred to buy a given number of shares at any price within the initial price range. Or the investor may submit the *limit bid* which means the bidder provides a price-quantity combination. Generally, investors can submit bids at any time until the book closes. The third step is the book-building process is determining the final price and the allocation of shares.[3]

IPO Pricing and First-Day Offering

The pricing of an IPO is a delicate balancing act. The lead underwriter has to worry about two different sets of clients—the company going public that wants to raise as much capital as possible, and the investors buying the shares who expect to see some immediate appreciation on their investment. The lead underwriter usually tries to price a deal so that the opening day price appreciation is about 15 percent. Of course, many hot Internet IPOs have risen much more than that of their first day. However, if the lead underwriter feels that the market may not be receptive to the offer price and the demand may be lacking, then the IPO offering may be postponed for a short time or for an indefinite period.

Once the offering price has been agreed to by the company and the lead underwriter—and at least two days after potential investors receive the final prospectus—an IPO is declared effective. This is usually done after the market closes, with trading in the new stock starting the next day. The lead underwriter is primarily responsible for ensuring smooth trading in a company's stock during those first few crucial days of public trading. Typically, the underwriter sells 115 percent of the issue at the offering price. If stock price goes up, it uses the overallotment option to cover its short position. If stock price goes down, it covers the overallotment option by buying stocks in the open market.

It has been found in an overwhelming number of studies that initially IPOs are underpriced. As Professor Dean LaBaron has pointed out, "A significant body of evidence indicates that on aggregate, IPOs have underperformed the market, typically 30 to 50 percent below comparable companies over three to five year periods."[4] For a "hot" IPO investors are generally willing to pay much more than the offering price and want more shares to be offered. The underwriters restrict the price and the amount of shares offered, thus causing a first-day hike that produces abnormal market returns. For example, the average first-day gain in initial public offerings managed by Morgan Stanley Dean Witter was 178 percent in early 2000 (through March 7), up from 24 percent in 1997.[5] Many of the other investment banks had similar first day gains..

The underlying imbalance manifests itself with "money being left on the table," i.e., the money the IPO firm forfeits on the first day of trading due to the underpricing of shares. This is the indirect cost to the IPO firm for going public, not associated with the direct cost of going public. In table 2.1 we have shown the aggregate amount of money "left on the table," along with the number of IPOs and average first-day returns during 1991-1999, all taken from Professors Tim Loughran and Jay Ritter's study.[6] Here money left on the table is defined as the closing market price on the first day of trading, minus the offering price, multiplied by the number of shares offered (excluding overallotment options) on a global basis. We find that as the number of IPOs increased by over 85 percent during 1991-1999, so also the amount left on the table that increased by 248 percent during the same period. The maximum value of the latter, of course, was in 1999 that was the "year of the IPOs." In that year the average first-day return, also, increased by 58.9 percentage points as compared to 1991. Here, "money left on the table" means less money raised from the IPO proceeds. When the IPO market started to melt down after March 2000, a lack of cash ended up killing many of the same companies.

The disparity between the first-day closing price and the offering price of the stocks was narrowed down considerably when the IPO market came back from the crash of 2001-2002. Companies issuing IPOs in 2003 had risen 13 percent on their first-day of trading, according to the data provided by the Thomson Financial, though that figure rose to about 16 percent if real-estate investment trusts were excluded. That was close to the figure from 1991 through 1994 that was generally considered a stable period for the IPOs when the first-day gains averaged between 9.8 percent and 12.8 percent, according to the calculation made by Professor Jay Ritter.

In the estimates of Thomson Financial, NASDAQ-listed IPOs had gained an average of 18.5 percent on their first days of trading, and 40.5 percent over their offering during the first three-quarters of 2003. By contrast, new stocks on the New York Stock exchange had 8.7

Table 2.1
Number of IPOs with Average First-Day Return
and Aggregate Amount Left on the Table

Year	Number of IPOs*	Average First Day Return	Aggregate Amount Left on the Table
1991	250	11.4%	$1.39 Billion
1992	338	9.9	1.65
1993	437	11.6	3.12
1994	319	8.6	1.37
1995	366	20.4	4.16
1996	570	16.0	6.43
1997	389	13.8	4.21
1998	266	21.8	4.93
1999	463	70.3	35.93

* Exclude IPOs with original file price range of less than $8, ADRs, unit trusts, Closed-end funds, REITS and partnerships.

percent, and were up 18 percent overall during the same period. That difference in performance could be explained by the size of the companies coming public. The nine companies that were listed in the NYSE in 2003 had raised an average of $422 million, while the 14 NASDAQ-listed IPOs had raised an average of $121 million, according to Thomson Financial. We should remember that the smaller deals are to be expected to post bigger gains as compared to the larger ones that would be hard to move too fast.

The question is: why are new issues so underpriced? Here we can adduce briefly several theories cited in financial literature:

- Winner's curse. Professor Kevin Rock (1986) had pointed out long time ago investors' demands are rationed for good firms and not for poor firms due to informed investors' participation in only good IPOs. Informed investors will bid only on those issues, while uninformed investors will pick both good and bad issues. In a good issue, both groups will compete and, hence, uninformed investors will get only partial allotment. But on bad issues, the only investors' bidding are the uninformed, and so the uninformed investors will receive their full allotment of bad IPOs. This is called a "winner's curse"—they receive a large amount of bad IPOs and a small amount of good IPOs. Thus underpricing gives the uninformed investors only normal return. They require underpricing as compensation for the risk of purchasing new issues.
- Monopsony. Professor David Baron (1989) had pointed out that a small number of underwriters following any particular industry allow the potential monopsony.
- Hype. Investor demand is often unusually heavy because of the hype surrounding an IPO and the strong selling effort employed by the underwriting syndicate. IPOs are viewed as publicity events, with the stellar gains ensuring that the companies got a good deal of media exposure.
- Reputation. Professors Franklin Allen and Gerald Faulhaver (1989) had pointed out that firms are able to access capital markets better in future if they "leave a good taste" in investors' mouth.
- Avoidance of lawsuits. Here the theory is that the IPO companies and underwriters discount initial price in order to avoid litigation for mis-representing overpriced stocks to shareholders.
- Censured distribution. Professor Judith Rund (1993) had advanced the hypothesis that perhaps underwriters correctly price the initial offerings, on average, but their stock stabilization efforts remove the downside risk, leading to average positive performance.
- Bandwagon effect. Professor Ivo Welch (1992) had pointed out that if investors pay attention to the IPO demand of other investors, band-wagon effects can create excessive demand for some offerings.

The Aftermarket and Lockup Expiration

The final stage of the IPO process begins twenty-five calendar days after the IPO debuts when the so-called "quiet period" ends. It is only after this period that the underwriters can comment on the valuation of the IPO and provide earnings forecast of the new company. The activities of the underwriters after initial public offerings are important for stabilizing the aftermarket price. As Professor Reena Aggarwal has pointed out, underwriters try to stabilize the aftermarket in three forms[7]: first, underwriters post a stabilizing bid to buy shares at a price not exceeding the offer price if the distribution of shares is not complete. This she calls "pure" stabilization. Second, underwriters initially sell shares in excess of the original amount offered, thus taking a short position prior to the offering that can be covered by exercising the overallotment option and/or by short covering in the aftermarket. In offerings where weak demand is anticipated, underwriters frequently take a naked short position by allocating more than 115 percent of the stated size of the offering. This form of price support may be called as "aftermarket short covering." Finally, underwriters may penalize members of the selling group whose customers frequently "flip" shares in the aftermarket by taking away their selling concession. This is generally referred to as a "penalty bid."

Professor Daniel J. Bradley, et al, have examined the expiration of the IPO "quiet period."[8] They have found that the analyst coverage was initiated immediately for 76 percent of the firms they studied, and almost always with a favorable rating. The firms with analyst coverage experienced much higher abnormal returns than firms without analyst coverage. Also, the abnormal returns were concentrated in the days just before the quiet period expired, and it was much larger when the coverage was initiated by multiple analysts. It is to be noted, however, that in July 2002, the SEC extended the "quiet period" from twenty-five calendar days to forty calendar days after an IPO is issued.

The lockup period is the time —usually 180 days—during which insiders (including management) are forbidden to sell their shares. However, the lead underwriter has the option of lifting the lockup period earlier. At the expiration of the lockup period, management as well as the board of directors of the IPO firms are free to sell their shares in the company. We may point out here that lockups serve several important purposes. They reassure the market that the key management people will work hard to shore up the stock price for at least for six months after the IPO. They also assure that the insiders will not be able to cash out in the case of bad news. And they strengthen the efforts of the underwriters to stabilize the price by temporarily controlling the supply of the IPO shares.

It is, thus, apparent that the people who handle and advise a company during the creation of the IPO are catalysts for the success of the firm's offering. To quote Professor Welch:

> It is important for entrepreneurs to hire someone independently who understands IPOs, preferably someone who understands IPOs in the same industry. Auditors, lawyers and underwriters all have interests conflicting with the entrepreneur's interests. The auditors want to make sure they do not get sued and bill as many hours as possible. The lawyers want to never state anything in writing for which later they can be held liable, and also be paid as many hours as possible. The underwriters want to do "the deal" under conditions as favorable to them as possible, including pricing the offering low so as to minimize their necessary selling effort. When negotiating with the underwriter, it is imperative that the firm runs the numbers itself first.[9]

Notes

1. See Judith Kauth, 2000, "Initial Public Offerings," www.About.com.
2. Chen, H-C, and J. R. Ritter, 2002, "The Seven Percent Solution), *Journal of Finance*, 55, 1105-1131.
3. See "Introduction," by T. Jenkinson and A. Ljungqvist, 2001, *Going Public*, Oxford University Press, pp. 17-19.
4. See D. LaBaron, 2001, "The Ultimate Investor," www. Deanlabaran.com.
5. Press Release by Morgan Stanley Dean Willer, 2001.
6. Loughran, T. and J. R. Ritter, 2002, "Why Don't Issuers Get Upset About Leaving Money on the Table in IPOs?" *Review of Financial Studies*, 15, 413-443.
7. Aggarwal, R., 2000, "Stabilization Activities by Underwriters After New Offerings," *Journal of Finance*, 55, 1075-1104.
8. Bradley, D. J., and B. D. Jordan, 2002, "All is not Quiet on the IPO Front," *Working Paper*, University of Kentucky, Lexington, KY.
9. The quotation is taken from Ivo Welch's *IPO Resource Page*, http;/Linux. agsm.ucla.edu/ipo.

References

Allen, F., and R. G. Faulhaver, 1986, "Signaling by Underpricing in the IPO Market," *Journal of Finance*, 23, 303-323.

Benveniste, L. M. and P. A. Spindt, 1989, "How Investment Bankers Determine the Offer Price and Allocation of New Issues," *Journal of Financial Economics*,24, 213-232.

Cornelli, F. and D. Goldreich, 2003, "Bookbuilding: How Informative is the Order Book?" *Journal of Finance*, 58, 1415-1443.

Ellis, K., R. Michaely, and M. O'Hara, 2000, "When the Underwriter is the Market Maker: An Examination of Trading in the IPO Aftermarket," *Journal of Finance*, 55, 1039-1074.

Hanley, K. W., 1993, "The Underpricing of Initial Public Offerings and the Partial Adjustment Phenomena," *Journal of Financial Economics*, 34, 213-230.

Field, L. C., and G. Hanka, 2001, "The Expiration of IPO Share Lockups," *Journal of Finance*, 56, 471-500.

Rock, K., 1986, "Why New Issues are Underpriced," *Journal of Financial Economics*, 15, 187-212.

Rund, J. S., 1993, "Underwriter Price Support and the IPO Underpricing Puzzle," *Journal of Financial Economics*, 34, 135-151.

Sherman, A. E., 2000, "IPOs and Long Term Relationship: An Advantage of Book Building," *Review of Financial Studies*, 13, 697-714.

3

The Mispricing and Flipping
of the Internet IPOS

There were over 200 Internet stocks in the securities markets in the year 2000 that were launched during the preceding five years. In 1999 alone, there had been well over fifty Internet IPOs. By providing access to the public markets, the IPO is both a channel of new capital to flow to the start-up companies and for the entrepreneurs to reap returns for their labor. It was the Internet IPOs that had fueled the fire of the information technology revolution in the late 1990s.

Today the overwhelming majority of financial economists believe that the IPOs were underpriced, that there was a "flipping" action among the early owners of stocks to sell them within a very short time and reap a lofty profit from that activity. But in the long run, many IPOs appeared to be overpriced, as Ritter (1991) and others had found. He found that in three years after going public, these firms underperformed significantly when compared with firms matched by size and industry. It provides evidence concerning Shiller's (1990) hypothesis that equity markets in general and the IPO market in particular, are subject to fads that affect the market price of stocks.

Hanley (1993) had found that stocks that were priced above the initial filing price range performed well on the first day of issuance, and stocks that were priced below the price range did poorly on the first day. More recently, Krigman, Shaw and Womack (1999) had examined the IPO phenomena, and had found that the first-day winners continued to be winners during the first year, and the first-day losers continued to be losers during the same time period. But the "extra-hot" IPOs performed worse over the future years. Also, the large traders "flipped" IPOs within a very short time that performed the worst in the future.

The objective of this chapter is to examine the IPO phenomenon anew, particularly the Internet IPOs which started in significant numbers in 1996 and virtually dried up after 2000, when the stock market in general went sour. There is a good deal of evidence that the IPOs were underpriced during this boom period of the NASDAQ stock market. Along with the general IPO markets, the Internet IPOs, too, became of little value after the boom market ended in 2000. Our study will examine this phenomenon as occurred during 1996-2000.

Our main objectives are to test whether the Internet IPOs were underpriced in the short run, and the nature and extent of the "flipping" phenomenon done by the institutional investors. Also, we want to examine the issue raised by Krigman, et al., that the first-day winners continued to outperform the market, and the first-day losers continue to lose over the first year. By examining the performance of these firms will provide some important clues whether the technology-driven "New Economy" is indeed a fad, or a phenomenon worth studying for its lasting impact in the society.

Data Sources and Methodology

The main data source for Internet IPOs was EDGAR OnLine—IPO Central, and the Securities Data Company (SDC) New Issues Database. Also, there are many web-sites now-a-days that contain data for Internet IPOs, such as www.financialweb.com, www.yahoo.com, and www.ipo.com, to name a few. All told, data for 200 Internet IPOs were collected covering the period 1996-2000.

The main methodology we followed to analyze the Internet IPOs was that of Krigman, et al. (1999). Following them, we had divided the IPOs into four groups: cold IPOs, where the first-day return was < =0 percent; cool IPOs where the first-day return was 0 percent < 10 percent; hot IPOs where the first-day return was 10 percent < 60 percent; and extra-hot IPOs where the first-day return was >60 percent. "Flipping" is defined as the immediate sale of IPO allocations back to the market or the underwriting syndicate, mainly by the institutional investors. We have calculated the flipping ratio as percentage of total shares sold in the first day, as well as the degree of flipping activities, such as low, medium or high percentage of immediate selling.

We have also employed the multiple regression model in order to find out the relationship between returns as the dependent variable, and various relevant variables as the independent variables. The multiple regression equation is of the form:

$$Y = a_0 + b_1X_1 + b_2X_2 + b_3X_3 + b_4X_4$$

Where:

Ys = Returns of different time periods
X_1 = Market capitalization ($million)
X_2 = Offering price ($)
X_3 = Shares offered ($ million)
X_4 = Day 1 opening price ($)

Following the Finance literature, we would expect the b-coefficients to be positive, except the first-day opening price to be inversely related with the returns.

The following are the formulas for the calculation of various return statistics:

1. First-Day Return = (First day close price - First day offering price) / First day offering price * 100

The first day return represents the percentage growth between the first day closing price and the offering price.

2. Second-Day Return = (Second day closing price - First day closing price) / First day closing price * 100

The second day return represents the percentage growth between the second day closing price and the first day closing price.

3. Third-Day Return = (Third day closing price - First day closing price) / First day closing price * 100

The third day return represents the percentage growth between third day closing price and the first day closing price.

4. One-Month Return = (One month closing price - First day closing price) / First day closing price * 100

The one-month return represents the percentage growth between the one-month closing price and the first day closing price.

5. Six-Month Return = (Six month closing price - First day closing price) /
                      First day closing price * 100

The six-month return represents the percentage growth between the six-month closing price and the first day closing price.

6. One-Year Return = (One year closing price - First day closing price) /
                     First day closing price * 100

The one-year return represents the percentage growth between the one-year closing price and the first day closing price.

Empirical Results

In table 3.1, we have shown the mean and median return statistics of the Internet IPOs during 1996-2000. Here we find that the mean of the first-day return was highest in 1999, and then fell off precipitously in 2000. That was also true for the second-day and third-day returns. But for the years 1996-1998, second-day returns were negative, which was also true for the third-day return for 1996. The one-month mean returns were good in 1998 and 1999, which was true for the six-month returns. Over all, 1998 had the best one-year return because the mean returns were negative in both 1999 and 2000, when the Internet bubble stated to burst.

In table 3.2, we have partitioned the IPO sample into cold, cool, hot, and extra-hot IPOs, following the methodology of Krigman, Shaw and Womack (1999). We have found that the first-day mean return of extra-hot IPOs was 121.5 percent, while that of cold IPOs it was −3.8 percent. But for one-month return it was only 6.9 percent for the extra-hot IPOs, while for the cold IPOs it was again −3.8 percent. For the six-month return, the mean was again high for the extra-hot IPOs, and positive for the cold IPOs. But the one-year return for the extra-hot IPOs was a moderate 12.3 percent and mere 1.4 percent for the hot IPOs, and both the cold and cool IPOs showed negative returns during the period covered by our study. Both the tables support the findings of Krigman et.al., that the first-day winners continue to be winners over the first year, and the first-day losers continue to be losers during the same period.

Table 3.3 shows the flipping activity by the institutional investors in various categories. In Panel A, we find that the stocks with high

Table 3.1
Daily, Monthly, and First-Year Return Statistics of Internet IPOs, 1996-2000

| | 1996 | 1997 | 1998 | 1999 | 2000 |
	n=7	n=15	n=23	n=85	n=52
First-Day Return					
Mean	12.97	4.93	20.29	206.1	6.03
Median	6.36	2.44	5.03	390.2	2.01
Second-Day Return					
Mean	1.31	1.32	3.12	15.57	-0.07
Median	-0.15	1.61	3.56	20.98	-2.18
Third-Day Return					
Mean	-3.56	0.56	1.27	3.27	-11.45
Median	-1.84	0.01	2.11	0.18	-17.84
One-Month Return					
Mean	1.08	-2.61	10.43	33.58	-10.58
Median	0.02	-7.16	9.75	59.83	-18.25
Six-Month Return					
Mean	12.10	46.40	101.04	5.67	-6.15
Median	-2.95	19.80	23.97	-3.47	-2.18
One-Year Return					
Mean	8.43	51.13	203.19	-59.24	-40.52
Median	-9.22	36.01	96.01	-43.66	-71.29

flipping ratios were held by the institutional investors in least amount as measured by the percentage of institutional shares to total shares offered. In Panel B, we find that there was a direct correlation between the amount of institutional shares as percentage of total shares offered, and the first-day performance of the Internet IPOs. Both the number and the percentage of institutional shares were lowest for the cold IPOs and highest for the extra-hot IPOs, reaching as high as 82 percent of the total for the latter category.

In table 3.4, we have shown the details of the returns partitioned by first-day performance and total flipping activities. Here, again, we find that, except for the cold IPOs for the first month, stocks with

Table 3.2
IPO Returns Partitioned by Mispricing

	Cold (<= 0 %) n=27	Cool (0%-10 %) n=23	Hot (10%-60%) n=59	ExtraHot (>60 %) n=73
First-Day Mean Return				
Mean	-3.8 %	5.3 %	41.2 %	121.5 %
Median	-1.6 %	4.6 %	37.9 %	101.6 %
One-Month Mean Return				
Mean	-3.8 %	2.9 %	8.3 %	6.9 %
Median	-2.8 %	1.4 %	4.2 %	5.4 %
Six-Month Mean Return				
Mean	2.9 %	-4.1 %	1.8 %	31.5 %
Median	1.9 %	-2.6 %	0.05 %	25.2 %
One-Year Mean Return				
Mean	-3.2 %	-9.4 %	1.4 %	12.3 %
Median	-2.1 %	-5.5 %	2.7 %	11.9 %
% Change From Filling Price				
Mean	3.5 %	11.2 %	29.4 %	93.6 %

Table 3.3
Institutional Investment by Flipping Activity

	Obs	Nos. of Inst. Holders		Inst. Shares as % of shares Offered at Opening Day	
		Mean	Median	Mean	Median
Panel A: Partitioned By Flipping Quartile					
High Flipping	87	51	43	59 %	56 %
Medium Flipping	56	59	50	71 %	66 %
Low Flipping	58	30	28	85 %	74 %
Panel B: Partitioned By Opening Day Performance					
Cold IPOs	71	24	22	52 %	51 %
Cool IPOs	49	39	31	61 %	57 %
Hot IPOs	33	48	40	75 %	66 %
Extra-Hot IPOs	47	60	56	82 %	71 %

Table 3.4
Returns Partitioned by First-Day Performance and Flipping Activity

	Cold IPOS n=27		Cool IPOs n=23		Hot IPOs n=59		Extra-Hot IPOs n=73	
	Mean	Median	Mean	Median	Mean	Median	Mean	Median
1-Month Size Adj. Returns By Day 1 Flipping Activity								
Low	-0.07%	-0.09%	8.7 %	9.1 %	46.1 %	42.5 %	217.8%	224.1 %
Medium	-9.1 %	-8.2 %	3.1 %	2.7 %	21.9 %	19.9 %	91.6 %	84.2 %
High	-28.6%	-21.3%	2.4 %	1.3 %	17.4 %	11.2 %	67.1 %	64.7 %
6-Month Size Adj. Returns By Day 1 Flipping Activity								
Low	9.8 %	8.7 %	5.9 %	6.3 %	82.3 %	76.3 %	109.3%	104.5 %
Medium	-5.6 %	-7.2 %	-3.1 %	-2.9 %	31.2 %	26.4 %	23.3 %	21.5 %
High	-35.3%	-31.1%	-11.5 %	-12.8 %	-0.09 %	-1.5 %	10.9 %	6.7 %
1-Year Size Adj. Returns By Day 1 Flipping Activity								
Low	6.4 %	5.8 %	23.4 %	21.7 %	13.4 %	11.7 %	67.9 %	62.1 %
Medium	-37.8%	-32.6%	-2.5 %	-2.1 %	-6.8 %	-5.9 %	11.7 %	10.2 %
High	-65.8 %	-60.9 %	-12.5 %	-10.9 %	-13.6 %	-13.2 %	-5.6 %	-4.3 %

low flipping ratios outperformed those stocks with both the median and high flipping ratios. Also, both the mean and median returns were much higher for the hot and extra-hot IPOs, than the cold and cool IPOs. But the return percentage came down considerably as the time progressed from one month to one year.

In table 3.5, we have run the multiple regression equations with the first-day, one-month, six-month and one-year returns as the dependent variables (Y), and market capitalization (X_1), offer price (X_2), shares offered (X_3), and day-1 opening price (X_4) as the Independent variables. We find that only the day-1 opening price was consistent and negatively associated with the return variables. Offer price was significant in two equations, but the signs were not consistent in all the equations. Market capitalization variable was significant only in the case of one-month return equation, but the shares offered variable was not significant at all in any of the equations. Also, except for the first-day return equation, relatively low R^2 values indicate weak association of the independent variables with the return variable of the equation.

Concluding Remarks

We have thus found that for the Internet stocks, the first-day mean return for the extra-hot IPOs was extremely high, but for the cold

Table 3.5
Multiple Regression Equations of Returns as the Dependent Variable

Dependent Variable (Y)	Intercept	Independent Variables				
		Market Capitalization (X_1)	Offer Price (X_2)	Shares Offered (X_3)	First Day Opening Price (X_4)	R^2
1-Day	0.0827	0.0003	-0.0684*	-0.0043	- 0.0640*	0.409
Return	(0.9408)	(0.4286)	(4.6849)	(0.2945)	(5.6001)	
1-Month	-0.0146	-0.0012*	0.0047	0.0246	-0.0057*	0.383
Return	(0.1648)	(1.5)	(0.7460)	(0.0147)	(2.2800)	
6-Month	0.1791	0.0096	0.0302**	-0.0110	0.0269*	-0.367
Return	(0.4925)	(1.0527)	(1.1527)	(0.1818)	(2.5619)	
1-Year	0.1850	-0.0024	0.0890*	0.0224	-0.0673*	0.314
Return	(0.3940)	(0.5714)	(2.6311)	(0.2868)	(4.9852)	

Standard Errors of the variables are in parentheses.
*5% level of significance
**10% level of significance

IPOs the return was negative. Also, stocks with high flipping ratios were held the least amount and stocks with the low flipping ratios were held the maximum by the institutional investors. Furthermore, only the first-day opening price was significantly associated with the return variable, although the relationship was negative during the period covered by our study.

References

Affleck-Graves, John, Shantaram Hedge, and Robert E. Miller, 1996, "Conditional Price Trends in the Aftermarket for Initial Public Offerings," *Financial Management* 25, 25-40.

Asquith, Daniel, Jonathan D. Jones, and Robert Kieschnick, 1998, "Evidence on Price Stabilization and Underpricing in Early IPO Returns," *Journal of Finance* 53, 1759-1773.

Carter, Richard B., and Frederick H. Dark, "Underwriter Reputation and Initial Public Offers: The Detrimental Effects of Flippers," *The Financial Review* 28, 279-301.

Hanley, Kathleen Weiss, 1993, "The Underwriting of Initial Public Offerings and the Partial Adjustment Phenomenon," *Journal of Financial Economics* 34, 231-250.

Krigman, Laurie, Wayne H. Shaw, and Kent L. Womack, 1999, "The Persistence of IPO Mispricing and the Predictive Power of Flipping," *Journal of Finance* 54, 1015-1044.

4

Post-Issue Operating Performance
of NASDAQ IPOs

Initial Public Offering (IPO) was an important part of the stock market bullishness in the 1990s. Although many IPOs were issued in the New York Stock Exchange, it was the NASDAQ market, however, which played a crucial role in this boom and took the lion's share of IPO issuance. The NASDAQ market became the harbinger of the new information technology where a large number of IPOs took part in implementing the change in manufacturing and service industries. They, in fact, become the face of the IT revolution.

In our study we have taken a fair sample of NASDAQ IPOs issued during the years covering 1990-2000. Our main objective is to examine the post-issue operating performance of these IPOs as undergone during the last bullish period in the United States securities markets. We have excluded from our sample of the Internet IPOs, mainly because we want to take out the speculative bubble created by these IPOs. Instead, we have concentrated on those NASDAQ IPOs that survived when the so-called "bubble" burst in the late 2000, and which showed strong promise of survival in the years ahead. Only by studying these IPOs can we find some kind of "permanency" in the turbulent stock market that we witnessed during 1990-2000.

Literature Review and Data Source

The IPO firms principally came into being after 1970. However, only a few firms then went through initial public offerings, as Jain and Kini (1994) in their sample of 682 IPO firms found only twelve IPOs that were issued before 1980. It was only after 1982 that the

IPO market took off, and exploded during the bullish stock market period of 1991-2000. Here the most important studies of IPO performance were conducted by Jay Ritter and his collaborators. Ritter (1991), and Loughran and Ritter (1995) documented severe underperformance of initial public offerings (IPOs) during the past twenty years. They had suggested that investors might systematically be too optimistic about the prospects of firms that were issuing equity for the first time.

The opposite evidence was posited by Brav and Gompers (1997) who investigated the long-run underperformance of the IPO firms in a sample of 934 venture-backed IPO firms from 1975-1992. They found that venture-backed IPOs outperformed nonventure-backed IPOs using equal weighted returns. They also found, applying Fama-French (1993) three-factor asset pricing model and other benchmark measures, that venture-backed companies did not significantly underperformed, while the smallest nonventure-backed firms did. Their conclusion is that underperformance is not an IPO phenomenon, that underperformance is a characteristic of small, low book-to-market firms regardless of whether they are IPO firms or not.

Degeorge and Zackhauser (1993) were the first ones who examined the operating performance of the IPO firms. But they had studied a special type of IPO firms, namely, reverse leveraged buyouts (LBOs). Jain and Kini's article (1994) was the most relevant regarding post-issue operating performance of the IPO firms. Here they investigated the change in operating performance of firms as they make the transition from private to public ownership. They found a significant decline in operating performance subsequent to the initial public offering. They also found a significant positive relationship between post-IPO operating performance and equity retention by the original entrepreneurs, but no relation between post-IPO operating performance and the level of initial underpricing. Interestingly, we have found the opposite relationship between the initial underpricing and post-issue operating performance of the IPOs as our regression analysis implied. Jain and Kini also found post-issue declines in the market-to-book ratio, price-earnings ratios, and earnings per share of the IPO firms they covered, in their study.

There are three reasons given in finance literature for IPO underperformance. First is the agency problem relating to a firm's going public from private management where there is a potential for increased agency costs, as explained by Jensen and Meckling (1976) in their seminal article. The second reason is that managers try to window-dress their accounting numbers before going public, so that the pre-IPO performance is overstated and post-IPO performance is understated. And the third explanation is that generally the companies time their issues to periods of unusually good performance levels, which may be difficult to maintain in future.

We will address the same question anew, i.e., the underperformance (or otherwise) of the NASDAQ IPOs. The following are the principal data sources for our IPO analysis of the 1990s:

- The IPO Reporter.
- Investment Dealers' Digests.
- Securities Data Company of Thomson Financial.
- www. Ipo.com
- www.yahoo.com
- www.hoovers.com
- Compustat Data file,

Among these sources, Securities Data Company has become the most prominent one. Then comes the Compustat Data file where we may find the archival data to calculate the long-run performance of the IPOs. The other sources in the Web sites just supplement the missing data not to be found elsewhere. We should remember in this context that the IPO data are still too scattered to be found in one prime source. It will take years to build a comprehensive database encompassing the universe of all IPOs. Here Jay Ritter's efforts to fill that void deserves our professional gratitude.

Empirical Findings

In table 4.1, we have shown the first-day return, second-day return and third-day return of our sample of NASDAQ IPOs, issued during 1990-2000. We find that the mean first-day return increased from 3.29 percent in 1990 to 76.61 percent in 2000—over twenty-two times jump in ten years. But the highest increase took place in 1999 during the so-called "bubble" year. However, the second-day mean return during the same period was negative—from 1.26 percent in 1990 to –0.46 percent in 2000. The same trend was evidenced in the mean third-day return—from 1.58 percent in 1990 to –2.45 percent in 1999, and -0.23 percent in 2000. Obviously, the speculative fervor of the first-day return of the NASDAQ IPOs cooled

Table 4.1
Initial Returns of NASDAQ IPOs, 1990-2000

Year		First-Day Return			Second-Day Return			Third-Day Return	
		Mean	Media n		Mean	Media n		Mean	Media n
1990		3.29	3.98		1.26	2.10		1.58	1.01
1991		1.34	1.59		(0.14)	0.80		(2.38)	0.80
1992		2.56	2.83		0.43	0.60		(1.53)	(0.95)
1993		3.57	3.02		(0.60)	(0.45)		(2.73)	(2.60)
1994		4.68	4.33		0.18	0.26		0.62	0.93
1995		7.45	6.92		(1.72)	(3.60)		(1.12)	(3.60)
1996		21.34	16.30		1.01	1.00		1.64	2.10
1997		20.33	10.00		1.11	1.70		3.27	4.50
1998		12.32	7.50		0.74	(1.80)		(7.32)	(5.90)
1999		84.15	48.20		(1.57)	(1.10)		(2.45)	(4.70)
2000		76.61	50.70		(0.46)	(1.60)		(0.23)	(1.10)

off in later days when the profit-taking took place and there was considerable sell-off by the institutional investors.

In table 4.2, we have calculated the one-month, six-month , and one-year return of the NASDAQ IPOs covered by our study for the period 1990-2000. While in 1990, the one-month return was 6.10 percent, and in 1999 it was 6.65 percent, in 2000, however, it was a paltry 0.12 percent, when the IPO market started to slide downward. Similarly, the six-month return in 1990 was −10.03 percent, but increased to 80.32 percent in 1998 and 29.97 percent in 1999, while turning into −64.37 percent in 2000. But the one-year return, while quite high to the tune of 31.83 percent in 1990, jumped to 52.12

Table 4.2
One-Month, Six-Month, and One-Year Returns of NASDAQ IPOs, 1990-2000

Year		One-Month Return		Six-Month Return		One-Year Return
		Mean		Mean		Mean
1990		6.01		(10.03)		31.83
1991		2.90		16.77		(36.56)
1992		(17.86)		(26.46)		80.32
1993		23.46		55.20		29.97
1994		2.76		(53.70)		(64.37)
1995		(34.45)		(44.50)		(68.20)
1996		8.02		31.83		(18.08)
1997		15.40		(36.56)		34.78
1998		(13.70)		80.32		(9.35)
1999		6.65		29.97		52.12
2000		0.12		(64.37)		44.84

percent in 1999, and 44.84 percent in 2000. It seemed that the IPO market was still "hot" at the end of 2000, and slowed considerably only in 2001, when the "bubble" collapsed totally and the IPO market was in a downward spiral.

In table 4.3, we have given the summary measures of one-month, six-month and one-year returns for 1990-1995 and 1996-2000 periods. We find that during 1990-1995, the mean post-issue one-month return was 1.67 percent, the mean six-month return was 4.28 percent, and the mean one-year return was 5.23 percent, respectively. This could be compared with the results for the 1996-2000 period when the mean one-month return was 3.29 percent, mean six-month return was 16.96 percent, and the mean one-year return was 19.97 percent, respectively. The notion that 1996-2000 was a phenomenal period for the IPO market was borne out by the fact that both the mean six-month and mean one-year return jumped by 296 percent and 282 percent, respectively, during the later period as compared to the earlier period of the bullish stock markets.

In table 4.4, we have shown the selected asset management ratios of the NASDAQ IPO sample firms during 1990-2000. While the mean inventory turnover ratio was 6.59 times in 1990, it jumped to 18.86 times in 2000. But the mean fixed asset turnover ratio declined considerably during the same period—from 13.60 times to 6.75 times. The decline was also prominent in the working capital turnover when in 1990 it was 2.07, but became negative in both

Table 4.3
Summary Returns of NASDAQ IPOs, 1990-1995 and 1996-2000 Periods

	Mean	Median
One-Month Return	1.67 %	1.83 %
Six-Month Return	4.28 %	4.12 %
One-Year Return	5.23 %	5.56 %
1996 – 2000		
One-Month Return	3.29 %	3.14 %
Six-Month Return	16.96 %	15.25 %
One-Year Return	19.97 %	20.38 %

Table 4.4

Selected Asset Management Ratios of NASDAQ IPOs, 1990 – 2000

Year	Inventory Turnover		Fixed Asset Turnover		Working Capital Turnover	
	Mean	Median	Mean	Median	Mean	Median
1990	6.59	6.39	13.60	9.55	2.07	2.04
1991	8.77	5.36	6.33	4.81	0.18	1.13
1992	7.64	5.48	5.48	5.76	2.00	1.76
1993	9.29	7.54	15.02	13.89	5.48	2.10
1994	14.22	13.11	14.24	12.75	4.39	2.21
1995	16.62	15.35	14.41	13.74	4.06	1.73
1996	16.73	15.98	11.58	10.06	13.36	12.17
1997	15.44	13.31	9.25	6.73	13.48	12.09
1998	14.70	13.64	6.53	4.88	(9.69)	(11.91)
1999	17.16	15.95	6.01	5.86	(4.03)	(3.14)
2000	18.86	17.17	6.75	5.66	1.08	1.03

1998 and 1999, and increased slightly in 2000. This deterioration of both fixed asset turnover and working capital turnover indicates that both sales and total assets of many NASDAQ companies started to shrink long before the stock price of these companies plummeted during 2000-2001.

In table 4.5, we have calculated the operating efficiency of these NASDAQ firms during 1990-2000. We find that the mean net income per employee in 1990 was 2.67 percent, but became negative in all the later years of 1997 to 2000. This is also true for net income per dollar of gross plant and equipment. That the vast majority of IPO firms had no net income can also be seen in average earnings per share statistics for these companies which were negative for all the years covered by our study. While the share price of these stocks soared during the last stock market boom, the net earnings were negative for almost all the IPO firms in the United States during 1990-2000.

In table 4.6, we have shown the leverage ratios for 1990-1995 and 1996-2000 periods, along with the entire decade of 1990-2000. While the debt/asset ratio and the debt/equity ratio in per-

Table 4.5

Net Income Per Employee, Net Income Per Dollar of Gross Plant and Equipment, and Average EPS

Year	Net Income Per Employee		Net Income Per Dollar of Gross Plant & Equipment		Average EPS	
	Mean	Median	Mean	Median	Mean	Median
1990	2.67	2.84	0.09	0.10	(0.06)	(0.02)
1991	8.56	2.29	0.54	0.47	(0.07)	(0.03)
1992	0.91	1.37	0.17	0.14	(0.08)	(0.07)
1993	(17.55)	(11.39)	(0.72)	(0.67)	(0.13)	(0.11)
1994	12.13	5.07	0.65	0.83	(0.09)	(0.08)
1995	10.59	4.45	0.70	0.44	(0.01)	(0.02)
1996	12.80	7.47	1.35	1.27	(0.16)	(0.15)
1997	(1.93)	(1.13)	(0.38)	(0.18)	(0.18)	(0.17)
1998	(6.64)	(6.04)	(1.80)	(1.36)	(4.07)	(3.93)
1999	(1.86)	(1.66)	(0.58)	(0.69)	(4.23)	(4.18)
2000	(19.03)	(18.99)	(8.21)	(7.98)	(1.23)	(1.19)

centage term was 5.38 percent and 11.98 percent, respectively, the former ratio showed a modest gain of 15.23 percent in 1996-2000, and the later ratio showed a modest decline during the same period. This clearly indicates that the NASDAQ bubble was mainly created by the issuance of equity issues, not by selling debt instruments.

In order to find out the causal relationship between the IPO return as the dependent variable, on the one hand, and various relevant variables as the independent variables, on the other, we have employed the multiple regression model for our data-set. Here the multiple regression equation is of the form:

Table 4.6

Leverage Ratios of the NASDAQ IPOs, 1990 – 2000

Periods	Debt/Asset Ratio	Debt/Equity Ratio
1990 – 1995	5.38 %	11.98 %
1996 – 2000	15.23 %	3.13 %
1990 – 2000	13.61 %	4.26 %

$$AR = a_0 + b_1 MC + b_2 OP + b_3 SO + b_4 FC$$

Where:

AR = Annual Return of different years;

MC = Market capitalization ($ million);

OP = Offer price ($);

SO = Shares offered (million);

FC = First-day closing price ($).

In table 4.7, we have shown the regression results. We find that only the first-day closing price was consistently and negatively associated with the annual returns. Offer price was significant in two of the three equations, but the signs were contradictory. Market capitalization was significant in one equation only, and the number of shares was not significant at all in any of these equations. Thus the significance of the FC variable indicates that the gulf between the offer price and the first-day closing price cut the profit of the IPO companies, particularly in the bullish years of the IPO market in the United States economy.

Concluding Remarks

Thus, although the mean first-day return was very high, the mean second-day and third-day returns were negative during 1990-2000 for the NASDAQ IPOs. Both the fixed asset turnover and working capital turnover were lower in 2000 from 1990. The average earn-

Table 4.7

Multiple Regression Equations of Annual Return as the Dependent Variable

Dependent	Independent Variables				
(Ars)	MC	OP	SO	FC	R^2
1990 Annual Return (AR1)	0.0003 (0.0007)	-0.0461* (0.0028)	-0.0042 (0.0127)	-0.0980* (0.0050)	0.440
1995 Annual Return (AR2)	0.0264* (0.0055)	0.0039 (0.0041)	0.0026 (0.1018)	-0.0322* (0.0005)	0.398
2000 Annual Return (AR3)	-0.0059 (0.0018)	0.0166** (0.0094)	0.0095 (0.0069)	-0.0810* (0.0374)	0.376

Standard errors of the independent variables are in parentheses.

* 5 %level of significance.

** 10 % level of significance.

ings per share were negative throughout, as the debt/asset ratio increased considerably during the later part of the 1990s. Here also, the first-day closing price was consistently and negatively associated with the annual returns.

References

Affleck-Graves, J., S. Hedge, and R. E. Miller, 1996, "Conditional Price Trends in the Aftermarket for Initial Public Offerings," *Financial Management*, 25-40.

Asquith, D., J. D. Jones, and R. Kieschnick, 1998, "Evidence on Price Stabilization and Underpricing in Early IPO Returns," *Journal of Finance*, 53, 1759-1773.

Brav, A. and P.A. Gompers, 1997, " Myth or Reality? The Long-Run Underperformance of Initial Public Offerings: Evidence from Venture and Nonventure Capital-Based Companies," *Journal of Finance, 52,* 1791-1821.

DEGeorge F. and R. Zackhouseer, 1993, " The Reverse LBO Decision and Firm Performance," *Journal of Finance*, 48, 1323-1348.

Fama, E. and K. French, 1993, "Common Risk Factor in the Returns on Stocks and Bonds," *Journal of Financial Economics*, 33, 3-56.

Ghosh, Arvin, 2005, "The Pricing and Performance of Internet IPOs," *Advances in Financial Planning and Forcasting*, News Series, 1, 27-36.

Jain, B.A. and O.Kini, "The Post-Issue Operating Performance of IPOs," *Journal of Finance, 49, 1699-1726.*

Jensen, M.C. and W. Mechling, 1976, "Theory of the Firm: Managerial Behavior, Agency Costs and Ownership Structure," *Journal of Financial Economics*, 3, 306-360.

Krigman, L., W. H. Shaw, and K. L. Womack, 1999, "The Persistence of IPO Mispricing and the Predictive Power of Flipping," *Journal of Finance*, 54, 1015-1044.

Loughran, T. and J.R. Ritter, 1995, " The New Issuer Puzzle," *Journal of Finance, 50,* 165-199.

Ritter, J.R., 1991, "The Long-Run Performance of Initial Public Offerings," *Journal of Finance*, 46, 3-27.

5

Pricing and Performance of the United States IPOs

The Initial Public Offerings (IPOs) had a very prominent role to play in the United States stock market boom of 1991-1999. Thousands of IPOs were launched during this period both in the New York Stock Exchange and in the NASDAQ market, the latter taking the important part in the information technology revolution of the 1990s. Also, the NASDAQ market spawned a large number of Internet IPOs many of which, unfortunately, became bankrupt in 2001-2002 when the bubble burst at the end of 2000. Our main purpose here is to examine the pricing and performance of the IPOs—issued both in the NYSE and NASDAQ markets—which shaped the U.S. economy decidedly during the last crucial decade.

Literature Review and Data Source

The IPO firms came into being principally after 1970. However, only a few firms then went through initial public offerings, as Jain and Kini (1994) in their sample of 682 firms found only twelve IPO firms that were issued before 1980. It was only after 1982 that the IPO market took off, and exploded during the bullish stock market period of 1991-2000. Here the most important studies of IPO performance were conducted by Jay Ritter and his collaborators. Ritter (1991), and Loughran and Ritter (1995) documented severe underperformance of initial public offerings IPOs) during the past twenty years. They had suggested that investors might systematically be too optimistic about the prospects of firms that were issuing equity to the public for the first time.

The opposite evidence was given by Brav and Gompers (1997) who examined the long-run underperformance of the IPO firms in a sample of 934 venture-backed and nonventure-backed IPO firms from 1975 to 1992. They found that venture-backed IPOs outperformed nonventure-backed IPOs using equal-weighted returns. They also found, applying Fama-French (1993) three-factor asset pricing model and other benchmark measures, that venture-backed companies did not significantly underperform while the smallest nonventure-backed firms did. Their conclusion is that underperformance is not an IPO phenomenon, and that underperformance is a characteristic of small, low book-to-market firms regardless of whether they are IPO firms or not.

Degeorge and Zackhauser (1993) were the first ones who examined the operating performance of the IPO firms. But they had studied a special type of IPO firms, namely, reverse leveraged buyouts (LBOs). Jain and Kini's article (1994) was the most relevant regarding post-issue operating performance of the IPO firms. They had investigated the change in the operating performance of firms as they made the transition from private to public ownership. They found a significant decline in operating performance subsequent to the initial public offering. They also found a significant positive relationship between post-IPO operating performance and equity retention by the original entrepreneurs, but no relation between post- IPO operating performance and the level of initial underpricing.

We will address the same question anew, i.e., the underperformance (or otherwise) of both the NYSE and NASDAQ firms. The following are the principal data sources for our IPO analysis covering the period 1990-2000:

- The IPO Reporter.
- Investment Dealers' Digest.
- Securities Data Company of Thomson Financial.
- Compustat Data File.

Empirical Findings

In table 5.1, we have shown the first three days of returns, and one month, six month and one year returns of the IPOs during 1996-2000—the heydays of the IPOs in the United States. Here we find that, while the mean first-day return was very high for both the NYSE and NASDAQ IPOs, they became negative for second and third days, but the Internet IPOs were still positive during this period. While the one-month return was negative for the NYSE IPOs, they were positive for the NASDAQ IPOs. The reverse was true for one-year return

Table 5.1
IPO Returns 1996 – 2000

Term Period	NYSE n = 300	NASDAQ n = 99	Internet N = 177	All IPOs n = 576
First day	11.97	63.33	90.28	15.24
Second day	-0.04	-0.40	3.85	0.37
Third day	-0.17	-0.18	2.79	0.21
One month	-0.01	8.11	19.18	2.43
Six month	6.09	-6.47	45.69	5.37
One year	11.49	-16.92	21.47	3.23

where the return of the NYSE IPOs was positive, but that of NASDAQ was negative. But both the Internet IPOs and All IPOs showed positive returns throughout the period, although the annual return was much less than the first-day return.

In table 5.2, we have divided the returns statistics into four groups: cold IPOs (returns <0), cool IPOs (returns 0 percent - < 10 percent), hot IPOs (10 percent - <60 percent), and very hot IPOs (returns > 60 percent), following their rates of returns during 1900 – 2000. We find that the returns of the cold IPOs that were negative in the first day remained so during the entire period. The returns of the cool IPOs and hot IPOs also were positive from the first-day returns to one-year returns. In all, the mean one-year return for "cold" IPOs was –49.18 percent, while for hot IPOs it was 32.93 percent during the 1990 – 2000 time period. Except for cold IPOs, the high returns of hot and very hot IPOs indicated the booming stock market of the last decade.

In table 5.3, we have shown the calendar year returns of the United States IPOs of our sample in the three main categories for 1991-2000. Here we find that in 1990, the mean return of the NYSE IPOs was 20.68 percent, but for the NASDAQ IPOs it was –18.08 percent, resulting in a return of 9.01 percent for all the IPOs covered by our study. In 1999—the so-called "bubble" year —it was 6.6 percent for the NYSE IPOs, 29.97 percent for the NASDAQ (without Internet) IPOs, 45.75 percent for the Internet IPOs, and 23.05 per-

Table 5.2
IPOs From 1990-2000—Cold, Cool, Hot, and Very Hot IPO Returns

	Cold IPO's <= 0 %	Cool IPO's 0 %- <10%	Hot IPO's 10% - < 60%	Very Hot IPO's > 60 %
First day				
Return	(5.74)	4.24	29.16	174.68
Mean	(3.20)	4.30	25.00	155.00
Median	92	91	178	115
N				
Second day				
Return	(3.97)	3.15	19.32	461.29
Mean	(1.70)	2.36	16.67	461.29
Median	355	201	49	1
N				
Third day				
Return	(7.17)	(3.58	20.58	130.32
Mean	4.10)	2.95	16.75	67.86
Median	371	160	67	8
N				
One month				
Return	(15.07)	4.58	26.25	121.50
Mean	(10.20)	4.30	22.40	101.52
Median	317	103	146	40
N				
Six month				
Return	(38.62)	4.80	29.68	209.51
Mean	(36.81)	4.60	27.30	125.90
Median	325	55	137	87
N				
One year				
Return	(49.18)	4.60	32.93	184.86
Mean	(48.75)	4.95	30.65	115.80
Median	340	32	114	103
N				

cent for all the IPOs sampled. But in 2000, they all came crusing down, being –1.37 percent for the NYSE IPOs, -64.37 percent for the NASDAQ IPOs, -73.44 percent for the Internet IPOs and –34.55 percent for all the IPOs, respectively.

In table 5.4, we have shown two measures of operating efficiency, namely, operating ratio (operating expenses / sales), and the index of the cash flows (1990 = 100). We find that the mean operating ratio for the NYSE IPOs in 1991 was 1.61 that went up to 1.82 in 2000. For the NASDAQ IPOs, on the other hand, it was 1.78 in 1991, but decreased slightly to 1.70 in 2000. The mean operating ratios for the Internet IPOs, the decline was more pronounced during this period, coming down from 1.43 in 1991 to 1.25 in 2000.

Table 5.3
Calendar Year Returns of All IPOs 1990-2000

Year	NYSE Mean	NASDAQ Mean	Internet Mean	All IPOs Mean
1990	20.68	(18.08)	-	9.01
1991	7.89	34.78	-	15.62
1992	62.51	(9.35)	-	40.88
1993	3.78	52.12	-	18.33
1994	13.52	44.84	-	22.95
1995	40.45	51.84	-	43.87
1996	42.83	31.83	39.67	39.56
1997	(3.59)	(36.56)	59.45	8.06
1998	(1.13)	80.32	184.87	70.71
1999	6.61	29.97	45.75	23.05
2000	(1.37)	(64.37)	(73.44)	(34.55)

Table 5.4
Operating Ratios and Growth of Cash Flows of the IPOs, 1991-2000

Year	Mean Operating Ratios			Annual Growth of Cash Flows (1990=100)		
	NYSE	NASDAQ	Internet	NYSE	NASDAQ	Internet
1991	1.61	1.78	-	49.01	177.16	-
1992	3.32	1.73	-	37.27	118.09	-
1993	1.86	1.71	-	51.20	79.97	-
1994	1.79	1.88	-	172.79	401.13	-
1995	1.76	1.67	-	107.51	471.72	-
1996	1.96	1.89	1.43	87.24	747.09	-
1997	1.63	.76	1.50	83.55	474.38	(3.10)
1998	2.58	1.43	1.51	100.24	409.53	(7.79)
1999	2.03	1.97	1.49	570.56	898.93	(31.38)
2000	1.82	1.70	1.25	918.48	950.59	(119.99)

As for the average annual growth of cash flows during this pe-riod, the index (1990 = 100) grew to 918.48 in 2000 for the NYSE IPOs, but for the NASDAQ IPOs, it jumped from 177.16 to 950.59 in 2000. For the Internet IPOs, on the other hand, the index was all negatives during 1997-2000, being −119.99 in 2000. All these IPOs lost money throughout the period, but the IPOs in NYSE and NASDAQ built up fixed assets and took hefty depreciation allow-ances to include in the calculation of their cash flows. The Internet IPOs, being asset-poor all along, compounded their deficits with negative incomes and very little depreciation allowances through-out the period covered in our study.

In order to explore the causal relationship between the IPO return as the dependent variable, on the one hand, and various relevant variables as the independent variables, on the other, we have employed the multiple regression model for our data-set. Here the multiple regression equation is of the following form:

$$AR = a_0 + b_1\ MC + b_2\ OP + b_3\ FC + b_4\ AS + b_5\ DR + b_6\ AL$$

where:

AR = Annual Return of different years;
MC = Market Capitalization ($million);
OP = Offer Price ($);
FC = First-day Closing Price ($);
AS = Asset Size ($);
DR = Debt Ratio (Total Debt/ Total Asset);
AL = Asset Leverage (Debt/ Stockholders' Equity).

In table 5.5, we have shown the regression results. Here we find that the first-day closing price (FC) was significantly associated with the annual returns. Offer price (OP) was significant only for the first-day return and the sign was negative, indicating that lower offer price was a contributing factor for the high first-day return. Asset size (AS) was significant for the longer periods of time, namely, six-month and one-year's returns. The debt ratios (DR) were significant in four out of six regression equations, but the signs were mixed. Asset leverage ratio (AL) was significant in two equations, namely, for the second-day and third-day equations, but not for the longer periods of time. Market capitalization (MC) was not significant at all in any of the six equations.

In table 5.6, we have taken the dummy variables to indicate whether the firms were belonging to the NYSE (dummy variable = 0) or to the NASDAQ (dummy variable = 1) market. Here we find again that the first-day closing price was significant in all the six equations. The offer price was significant in the first-day return only. Again, the asset size was significant for the longer period of time, namely returns for six- month and one year. The debt ratio was significant again in four out of six equations, but the signs again were mixed. Asset leverage was significant only in two equations—for the first-day and second-day returns. But the market capitalization variable was not significant at all in any of the equations. The dummy variable, however, was significant for relatively longer period, not for the shorter period of time.

Table 5.5
Multiple Regression Equation of IPO Return in the Dependent Variable
(Without Dummy Variables)

Dependant Variable	Independent Variables						R^2
	MC	OP	FC	AS	DR	AL	
First Day Return	0.006 (0.213)	-0.318* (-5.431)	0.106 (1.814)	-0.002 -0.063	0.005 (0.200)	0.013 (0.521)	.669
Second Day Return	0.046 (0.585)	0.019 (0.139)	0.040* (1.304)	-0.057 (0.780)	0.118* (1.839)	0.174* (2.687)	.425
Third Day Return	-0.003 (-0.035)	-0.112 (-0.799)	0.149* (1.331)	-0.020 (-0.265)	0.036* (1.553)	0.207* (3.197)	.491
One Month Return	-0.029 (-0.356)	-0.098 (-0.687)	0.135* (1.501)	-0.015 (-0.197)	-0.037 (-0.561)	0.062 (0.942)	.393
Six Month Return	0.042 (0.434)	-0.124 (-0.641)	0.030** (1.159)	0.203* (2.001)	-0.124* (-1.584)	-0.007 (-0.079)	.368
One Year Return	0.037 (0.447)	0.058 (0.396)	0.201* (1.461)	0.102** (1.334)	0.054 (0.805)	-0.032 (-0.479)	.389

t values are in parenthesis
*   5 % level of significance
**   10 % level of significance

Table 5.6
Multiple Regression Equation of IPO Return in the Dependent Variable
(With Dummy Variables)

Dependant Variable	Independent Variables							R^2
	MC	OP	FC	AS	DR	AL	Dummy	
First Day Return	0.007 (0.232)	-0.314* (-4.681)	0.204* (3.803)	-0.001 -0.043	0.006 (0.256)	0.012 (0.506)	0.008 (0.305)	.639
Second Day Return	0.042 (0.534)	0.005 (0.136)	0.066* (1.483)	-0.061 (0.826)	0.108* (1.650)	0.176* (2.716)	-0.053 -(0.771)	.553
Third Day Return	-0.002 (-0.023)	-0.106 (-0.737)	0.143* (1.450)	-0.019 (-0.252)	0.038* (1.577)	0.207* (3.173)	0.013 (0.183	.494
One Month Return	-0.018 (-0.220)	-0.029 (-0.197)	0.062* (1.453)	-0.005 (-0.063)	-0.009 (-0.031)	0.056 (0.852)	0.149* (2.153)	.438
Six Month Return	0.042 (0.434)	-0.124 (-0.641)	0.030** (1.129)	0.203* (1.001)	-0.124* (-1.584)	-0.007 (-0.079)	0.179* (1.938)	.502
One Year Return	0.031 (0.378)	0.014 (0.090)	0.155* (1.198)	0.094** (1.235)	0.033* (1.483)	-0.027 (-0.406)	0.098** (1.385)	.445

t values are in parenthesis
*   5 % level of significance
**   10 % level of significance

Concluding Remarks

We have thus found that the average first-day return for all kinds of IPOs was over 15 percent during 1990-2000. But for the cold IPOs it was negative, while for the hot IPOs it was very high throughout the time period. For 1990, the mean return for all IPOs was over 9 percent, but in 1999, it was over 23 percent, and in 2000 it was negative for all IPOs. The mean operating ratio for the NYSE IPOs went up in 2000 from 1990, but for the NASDAQ IPOs it came down during the same period. But the average growth of cash flows went up for both the groups in 2000 as compared to 1990. Here the regression results show a consistent positive association between the first-day closing price and the return statistics.

References

Affleck-Graves, J., S. Hedge, and R. E. Miller, 1996, "Conditional Price Trends in the Aftermarket for Initial Public Offerings," *Financial Management*, 25-40,

Asquith, D., J. D. Jones, and R. Kieschnick, 1998, "Evidence on Price Stabilization and Underpricing in Early IPO Returns," *Journal of Finance*, 53, 1759-1773.

Brav, A. and P.A. Gompers, 1997, "Myth or Reality? The Long-Run Underperformance of Initial Public Offerings: Evidence from Venture and Nonventure Capital-Based Companies," *Journal of Finance, 52,* 1791-1821.

DeGeorge F. and R. Zackhouseer, 1993, "The Reverse LBO Decision and Firm Performance," *Journal of Finance*, 48, 1323-1348.

Fama, E. and K. French, 1993, "Common Risk Factor in the Returns on Stocks and Bonds," *Journal of Financial Economics*, 33, 3-56.

Ghosh, Arvin, "Post-Issue Operating Performance of NASDAQ IPOs," *Journal of Business and Economic Research*, 1, 37-42.

—————————, 2005, "The Pricing and Performance of Internet IPOs," *Advances in Finanaical Planning and Forecasting*, New Series, 1, 27-36.

Jain, B.A. and O.Kini, "The Post-Issue Operating Performance of IPOs," *Journal of Finance, 49, 1699-1726.*

Jensen, M.C. and W. Mechling, 1976, "Theory of the Firm: Managerial Behavior, Agency Costs and Ownership Structure," *Journal of Financial Economics*, 3, 306-360.

Krigman, L., W. H. Shaw, and K. L. Womack, 1999, "The Persistence of IPO Mispricing and the Predictive Power of Flipping," *Journal of Finance*, 54, 1015-1044.

Loughran, T. and J.R. Ritter, 1995, " The New Issuer Puzzle," *Journal of Finance, 50,* 165-199.

Ritter, J.R., 1991, "The Long-Run Performance of Initial Public Offerings," *Journal of Finance*, 46, 3-27.

6

Pricing and Long-Run Performance of Venture-Backed and Nonventure-Backed IPO

Initial public offerings (IPOs) were the most prevalent form of securities issuance to raise capital firms wanting to go public during the last decade (1990-2000) in the United States. The IPO phenomenon got a tremendous boost during the late 1990s by the popularity of the Internet stocks. Unfortunately, with the stock market downturn that taken place after the spring of 2000, many of these stocks had succumbed to the market pressure and had gone out of the market. Many well-established companies in the United States had also taken resort to the IPO market that are still in business and some are, in fact, thriving. Although technology-heavy NASDAQ stock market had the largest number of IPO firms, the New York Stock Exchange(NYSE) also had its share of the IPOs which were not insignificant at all in number.

Along with the regular IPOs came the IPOs backed by venture capitalists, who specialized in financing promising startup companies and bringing them public. They were the ones that substantially provided much-needed capital for the new public firms that were less dependent upon solely public-supported capital. It is to be noted here that since 1990, one out of every three IPOs was backed by venture capital, as data compiled by the Securities Data Company of Thomson Financial disclosed.

In this paper, we have addressed the question whether venture-backed IPOs perform better than the nonventure-backed IPOs. For that, we have taken the time period 1990-2000—a period of exceptional IPO growth, venture-backed and nonventure-backed alike. We have taken a sample of IPO firms, selected randomly both from the NYSE and NASDAQ stock market. For the regression analysis to explore the causal relationship, however, we have taken the data of the NYSE IPOs only, because these firms were better financed and adhered to higher standards.

Literature Review and Data Source

The underpricing of the IPOs in the short-run and their underperformance in the long-run are the general conclusions of most of the IPO studies regarding pricing and performance. The seminal articles by Jay Ritter (1991), and Longhran & Ritter (1995), as well as the review article by Ritter and Welch (2002) had discussed in detail these underpricing and long-run underperformance phenomena, particularly in the light of different econometric methodology and differing sample periods. Ritter and Welch also raised the question that nonrational explanations and agency conflicts might play an important part, especially during the so-called "bubble" period of late 1990s. They have also adhered to the view that share allocation and subsequent ownership of stocks should also be considered in future research of IPO pricing.

The contrasting evidence was advanced by Brav and Gompers (1997 in this regard. They had investigated the long-run underperformance of the IPO firms after partitioning them into venture-backed and nonventure-backed IPOs issued during the period of 1975-1992. They had found that venture-backed IPOs outperformed nonventure-backed IPOs using equal-weighted return. Also, value-weighting had significantly reduced performance differences and had substantially reduced underperformance for nonventure-backed IPOs in their sample. In tests using comparable benchmarks and the Fama-French (1993) three-factor asset pricing model relating to market return, size and book-to-market ratio, they also found that venture-backed IPOs did not significantly underperformed while the smallest nonventure-backed IPOs did.

Brav and Gompers had found that underperformance in the nonventure-backed sample was driven primarily by small issuers, i.e., those with market capitalization of less than $50 million. Underperformance, however, was not an IPO effect. Similar size and book-to-market firms that had not issued equity performed as poorly as IPOs in their sample. As small nonventure-backed IPOs are more likely to be held by individuals, investor sentiment plays a crucial role in their relative underperformance. These investors are more likely to be swayed by fads or lack of complete information. Venture-backed IPOs, on the other hand, have superior knowledge about the potential of startup firms they finance.

Barry, Muscarella, Peavy and Vetsuypens (1990), and Megginson and Weiss (1991) have found evidence that markets react favorably to the presence of venture capital financing at the time of an IPO. The latter researchers have also found that individuals, who are potentially more susceptible to fads and popular sentiments, hold a larger fraction of shares after the IPO for nonventure-backed firms. Also, venture capitalists stay on the board of directors long after the IPO and may continue to provide access to capital that nonventure-backed IPOs lack. Hoshi, Kashyap and Scharfstein (1991) have pointed out that because venture capitalists generally provide access to top-tier national investment and commercial bankers, they may partly overcome informational asymmetries that are associated with startup companies. Moreover, venture capitalists may have a hand in selecting management team that help the firm perform better in the long run.

More recently, Hellman and Puri (2002) have found that venture capital is related to a variety of professionalization measures, such as human resource policies, the adoption of stock option plans and the hiring of a marketing VP. Venture-capital backed IPOs are also more likely and faster to replace the founder of the company with an outside CEO, both in situations that appear adversarial and those mutually agreed upon. Their evidence also suggests that venture capitalists play roles over and beyond those of traditional financial intermediaries.

The following are the principal data sources for our study:

- The IPO Reporter.
- Investment Dealers' Digests.
- Securities Data Company of Thomson Financial.
- *www.Ipo.com*
- *www.yahoo.com*
- *www.hoovers.com*
- Compustat Data File.

Empirical Findings

In table 6.1, we have shown the total number of all IPOs and all venture-backed IPOs issued during 1990-2000. We find that out of the total of 4,566 IPOs, fully 1,672 or 36.62 percent of all IPOs were venture-backed.during this period. For all IPOs, they were issued in large number from 1992, reaching the maximun in 1996 when the number was 707, and 1993 coming next to it when 540 IPOs were issued. For the venture-backed IPOs, 1996 was also the best year when 233 IPOs of this nature were issued. The year 1998, however, was the lean year for the venture-backed IPOs that again took up speed in 1999 and 2000 when the numbers of all IPOs were still high, even when the stock market started to slacken off after March 2000.

In table 6.2, we have calculated for our sample of 237 IPO firms, the returns of different selected periods for venture-backed and nonventure-backed IPOs issued in the New York Stock Exchange (NYSE) between 1990 and 2001. Here we find that, except for the second-day return, the returns for all other periods were higher for the venture-backed IPOs as compared to the nonventure-backed IPOs. Although the difference in return between the two groups was slight for the first day, it was more pronounced for one-month, six-month and one-year returns. It is interesting to note that the first-day return for both types of firms was the highest, falling precipitously for second-day and third-day returns. This indicates that in the short-run, IPOs were underpriced for both the venture-backed and nonventure-backed firms. The one-year return for the nonventure-backed IPOs, although much lower in return than the venture-backed IPOs, showed modest gain as compared to the previous months.

Table 6.1
Numbers of Issues of All IPOs and Ventured-Backed IPOs, 1990-2000

Year	All IPOs	Ven-Backed IPOs
1990	108	37
1991	259	109
1992	415	154
1993	540	194
1994	441	127
1995	464	158
1996	707	233
1997	484	116
1998	295	71
1999	473	251
2000	380	222

Source: SDC of Thomson Financial, covering 1990 – 2000

Table 6.2
NYSE Returns for Venture-and Non Venture-Backed IPOs 1990-2001

	Venture			Non Venture		
	Mean	**Median**	**Standard Deviation**	**Mean**	**Median**	**Standard Deviation**
	n=76	*n=76*	*n=76*	*n=161*	*n=161*	*n=161*
First Day Return	13.2 %	9.7 %	16.2 %	13.6 %	6.9 %	22.2 %
Second Day Return	-0.4 %	-0.1 %	5.2 %	0.6 %	0.2 %	5.3 %
Third Day Return	0.1 %	-0.5 %	6.7 %	0.4 %	0.1 %	6.8 %
One Month Return	2.5 %	1.4 %	15.2 %	-1.0 %	-0.9 %	12.8 %
Six Month Return	5.2 %	2.2 %	18.7 %	2.7 %	0.6 %	19.8 %
One Year Return	10.3 %	7.5 %	22.6 %	6.3 %	-4.5 %	24.6 %

Table 6.3 shows the returns of the same selected periods for the venture-backed and nonventure-backed IPOs issued in the NASDAQ stock market during 1990-2001. Here we also find that the returns of the venture-backed IPOs were higher than the nonventure-backed IPOs for all the time periods covered by our study. The first-day return of the venture-backed IPOs was almost double as compared to the nonventure-backed IPOs, while for the entire year it was almost triple as compared to the latter group. Also, the first-day re-

Table 6.3
NASDAQ Returns for Venture-and Nonventure Backed IPOs 1990-2001

	Venture			Non Venture		
	Mean	**Median**	**Standard Deviation**	**Mean**	**Median**	**Standard Deviation**
	n=76	*n=76*	*n=76*	*n=133*	*N=133*	*n=133*
First Day Return	65.27 %	38.40 %	77.32 %	35.86 %	24.20 %	65.56 %
Second Day Return	-0.39 %	-2.44 %	10.05 %	-0.67 %	-0.59 %	9.07 %
Third Day Return	-2.14 %	-3.20 %	12.40 %	-4.69 %	-2.99 %	12.37 %
One Month Return	5.51 %	1.31 %	41.48 %	3.45 %	1.60 %	42.58 %
Six Month Return	24.36 %	18.05 %	6.00 %	21.41 %	3.20 %	23.81 %
One Year Return	39.16 %	26.80 %	25.23 %	14.59 %	9.41 %	58.02 %

turns for both groups were much higher for IPOs belonging to the NASDAQ stock market when compared with those belonging to the NYSE, which was also true for the one-year return. The technology-heavy NASDAQ market showed much higher returns where the majority of the IPOs were issued during 1990-2001.

In table 6.4, we have calculated the operating ratios as well as the growth of cash flows for these two types of IPOs issued in the New York Stock Exchange during 1991-2001. Here the results were mixed and we see no clear pattern for these two groups of IPOs. As for mean operating ratios, they were higher for the nonventure-backed IPOs in most of the years, while for the annual growth of cash flows, venture-backed IPOs did better in most of the years. It is interesting to note that in 1999—the so-called "bubble year"—growth of cash flows virtually exploded for both the groups. But here also, the growth of cash flows for the venture-backed IPOs was more than double as compared to the nonventure-backed IPOs.

In table 6.5, we have shown the mean operating ratios and the growth of cash flows for these two types of IPOs issued in the NASDAQ stock market during 1994-2001. Here also, the result was mixed for the mean operating ratios as they were higher for the venture-backed IPOs in only four out of eight years. Similarly, the annual growth of cash flows was also higher in four out of eight years covered by our study. But the growth rate of cash flows started to go

Table 6.4
Venture-Backed vs. Nonventure-Backed Operating Ratios and Growth of Cash
Flows of the IPOs, 1991-2001, NYSE Firms

Year	Venture		Non Venture	
	Mean Operating Ratios	Annual Growth of Cash Flows(%)	Mean Operating Ratios	Annual Growth of Cash Flows(%)
1991	0.66	1.3	0.56	35.7
1992	0.58	9.9	0.57	8.2
1993	0.67	12.5	0.77	10.8
1994	0.66	50.1	0.78	46.4
1995	0.57	100.4	0.53	75.0
1996	0.68	182.2	0.51	27.7
1997	0.52	74.7	0.79	42.3
1998	0.68	103.3	0.72	78.9
1999	0.67	1843.3	0.69	785.4
2000	0.58	467.0	0.67	368.0
2001	0.56	144.3	0.66	126.5

down in both 2000 and 2001for both types of IPOs. It showed that the IPO market had cooled down during these years, as the mean operating ratios started to climb up—another sign of increased cost in running the operations during the later years.

We have also employed the OLS regression model in order to explore the causal relationship between the IPO return as the dependent variable, and various relevant variables as the independent variables, for both the data-sets of venture-backed IPOs and nonventure-backed IPOs. The multiple regression equation is of the form:

$$AR = a_0 + b_1 \, FC + b_2 \, OP + b_3 \, SO + b_4 \, MC$$

Where:

    AR = Returns of different periods;

    FC = First-day closing price ($);

    SO = Shares offered (million);

    MC = Market capitalization ($ million).

In table 6.6, we have shown the regression results for venture-backed IPOs listed in the New York Stock Exchange (NYSE). We find that only the first-day closing price (FC) was negatively and significantly associated with the return variables in five out of six equations. Offer price (OP) was significant in two out of six equations, but the signs were contradictory. Shares Offered (SO) was significant only for the first-day return equation, as was Market capitalization (MC). Thus the significance of the FC variable indicates

Table 6.5

Venture vs. Nonventure Operating Ratios Growth of the Cash Flows of the IPOs, 1994-2001 NASDAQ Firms

Year	Venture		Non Venture	
	Mean Operating Ratios	Annual Growth of Cash Flows	Mean Operating Ratios	Annual Growth of Cash Flows
1994	0.49	3.42	0.33	-0.13
1995	0.41	23.07	0.48	2.08
1996	0.40	6.69	0.23	1.34
1997	0.49	7.86	0.40	14.09
1998	0.45	18.81	0.71	15.15
1999	0.30	7.08	0.56	9.74
2000	0.61	-49.14	0.67	-15.89
2001	0.74	-44.27	0.69	-5.86

Table 6.6
Multiple Regression Equations of Returns as the Dependent Variable
(Ventured-Backed IPOs)

Dependent	Independent Variable					
(Ars)	FC	OP	SO	MC	R^2	F Ratio
First Day Return (AR1)	-3.044* (-7.477)	-3.225* (-4.659)	-0.349* (-1.953)	0.751* (3.535)	0.450	5.962
Second Day Return (AR2)	1.101** (-1.369)	1.398** (1.500)	0.173 (0.230)	-0.611 (-0.683)	0.117	3.594
Third Day Return (AR3)	-0.941* (-1.798)	0.936 (1.022)	0.681 (0.914)	-0.848 (-0.959)	0.138	3.722
First Month Return (AR4)	0.364 (0.471)	-0.267 (-0.274)	-0.009 (-0.012)	-0.032 (-0.034)	0.223	4.105
Six Month Return (AR5)	-1.357* (-1.909)	1.527 (1.700)	0.197 (0.269)	-0.544 (-0.628)	0.271	4.927
One Year Return (AR6)	-0.521* (-2.683)	0.646 (0.671)	-0.312 (-0.398)	0.012 (0.013)	0.248	4.224

Standard errors of the independent variables are in percentages
* 1 % level of significance
** 5 % level of significance

the underpricing of the IPOs, particularly on the first day when the IPOs were offered to the public for the first time.

In table 6.7, we have shown the regression results for nonventure-based IPOs issued in the NYSE. Here we also find that the only the first-day closing price (FC) was negatively and consistently associated with the return variables in all the six equations. Offer price (OP) was negatively significant in first three of the six equations. Shares offered (SO) was significant (negatively) only for the one-year return equation as the dependent variable, as market capitalization (MC) was significant (positively) for the first-day return equation as the dependent variable. Both the R^2 and F-ratios indicate the relevancy of the equations, following the methodology of OLS regression model.

Concluding Remarks

We have found that the returns of the venture-backed IPOs were higher than the nonventure-backed IPOs. The same was true for the growth rate of cash flows. And the first-day returns of both the groups were higher than any other time periods. Here also, only the first-day closing price was significantly and negatively associated with

Table 6.7
Multiple Regression Equations of Annual Returns as the Dependent Variable
(Nonventured-Backed IPOs)

Dependent	Independent Variable					
(Ars)	FC	OP	SO	MC	R2	F Ratio
First Day Return (AR1)	-1.444* (8.776)	-1.004* (-2.156)	0.167 (0.697)	0.209* (1.813)	0.389	8.190
Second Day Return (AR2)	-0.843* (-4.629)	-0.845* (-4.306)	-0.108 (0.190)	0.197 (0.160)	0.352	6.506
Third Day Return (AR3)	-0.788* (-4.405)	-0.690* (-3.338)	0.090 (0.150)	-0.144 (0.225)	0.281	4.687
First Month Return (AR4)	0.197** (-1.682)	-0.013 (-0.045)	-0.136 (-0.196)	0.205 (0.785)	0.301	3.370
Six Month Return (AR5)	0.237** (-1.358)	0.150 (0.622)	-0.135 (0.193)	0.147 (0.196)	0.239	3.281
One Year Return (AR6)	-0.458* (-2.178)	-0.034 (-0.149)	-1.097** (-1.674)	1.233 (1.755)	0.236	3.894

* 1 % level of significance
** 5 % level of significance

most return statistics. Overall, the venture-backed IPOs performed better than the nonventure-backed IPOs during the period covered by our study.

References

Barry, C., C. Muscaralla, J. Peavy, and M. Vetsuypens, 1990, "The Role of Venture Capital in the Creation of Public Companies: Evidence from the Going-Public Process," *Journal of Financial Economics*, 27, 447-476.

Brav, A. and P.A. Gompers, 1997, "Myth or Reality? The Long-Run Underperformance of Initial Public Offerings: Evidence from Venture and Nonventure Capital-Based Companies," *Journal of Finance,* 52, 1791-1821.

Fama, E., and K. French, 1993, "Common Risk Factors in the Returns of Stocks and Bonds," *Journal of Financial Economics*, 33, 3-55.

Ghosh, Arvin, 2003, "Post-Issue Operating Performance of NASDAQ IPOs," *Journal of Business and Economic Research*, 1, 37-42.

Hellman, T., and M. Puri, 2002, "Venture Capital and the Performance of Start-Up Firms: Empirical Evidence," *Journal of Finance*, 58, 169-197.

Hoshi, T., A. Kashyap, and D. Scharfstein, 1991, "Corporate Structure, Liquidity, and Investment," *Quarterly Journal of Economics,* 106, 33-60.

Loughran, T., and J. R. Ritter, 1995, "The New Issue Puzzle," *Journal of Finance*, 50, 165-199.

Megginson, W., and K. Weiss, 1991, ""Venture Capitalist Certification in Initial Public Offerings," *Journal of Finance*, 46, 879-903.

Ritter, J. R., 1991, "The Long-Run Performance of Initial Public Offerings," *Journal of Finance*, 46, 3-27.

Ritter, J. R., and I. Welch, 2002, "A Review of IPO Activity, Pricing, and Allocations," *Journal of Finance*, 57, 1795-1828.

7

Pricing and Operating Efficiency
of Venture-Backed and Nonventure-Backed
Internet IPOs

Initial Public Offerings (IPOs) were the most popular form to raise new capital in the United States during the last decade (1990-2000). Thousands of companies went public for the first time, particularly in the technology-heavy NASDAQ stock market. Along with the regular IPOs came to Internet IPOs backed by the venture-capitalists, who specialize in financing promising start-up companies and bringing them public. More than half of the Internet IPOs were backed by the venture-capitalists during 1996-2001. For example, in 1998 venture-capitalists put $13.7 billion into 2,023 start-ups, up from $2.5 billion invested in 627 companies in 1994. In 1999 alone, Internet companies received nearly $20 billion in venture capital funding. As a matter of fact, hardly there was a successful Internet IPO in that year that did not receive funding from at least one big-name venture capitalist.

It was the Internet stocks that fueled the IPO outburst in the late 1990s. In 1991 the World Wide Web (WWW) was born when the new HTML code let programmers combine words, pictures and sound on Web pages. When in 1993, Marc Andressen and fellow University of Illinois students developed *Mosaic* to browse the web effectively, the number of users grew by leaps and bound at year's end. Within a very short time, web-based Internet browsing came into being and the online business was launched. It was online trading, in turn, that helped give rise to the volatile first-day and after-market performances for the Internet IPOs. And the significance of the Internet in reshaping both the United States and the world economy was enormous. It has changed such businesses as the selling of airline tickets and the distribution of financial service products, among many others. It ushered in the information technology we know to-day.

The Internet stocks took off when the first Web browser Netscape Communications (NSCP) came into being in 1995. It went public on August 1 of that year and its share prices soared 108 percent on its first day. In 1996, Yahoo went public, and the stock market value of the company was nearly $1 billion within a year. Then in 1997, the first e-commerce company Amazon.com went public. In 1998, during its first half, demand for the IPO stocks were so robust that on average forty-four new issues a month were floated. Since then, the Internet stock had dominated the IPO market until March 2000, when the whole stock market in the United States took a nosedive, so to speak, until the recovery process got started in 2003.

In this paper, we have addressed the question whether the venture-backed Internet IPOs performed better than the nonventure-backed Internet IPOs during 1996-2001. We have taken a sample of 117 Internet firms selected randomly, covering both the New York Stock Exchange and the NASDAQ stock market. Our objective here is to examine the pricing performance and operating efficiency of both the venture-backed and nonventure-backed Internet IPOs during the period covered by our study. By probing into these performance measurements of the Internet IPOs, we hope to shed new light into the controversy found in the Finance literature, that in general, the venture-backed IPOs performed better than the nonventure-backed IPOs during the past decade.

Literature Review and Data Source

Professor Jay Ritter (Ritter, 1991) and later Ritter and Professor Ivo Welch (Ritter & Welch, 2002) had found that the United States IPOs were underpriced in the short run and underperformed in the long run, suggesting that investors might systematically be too optimistic about the prospects of firms that were issuing equity for the first time. They had also found that the long-run performance of the IPOs was not only sensitive to the choice of econometric methodology, but also to the choice of the sample period. Also, the asymmetric information theories would unlikely be the primary determinant of fluctuations in IPO activity and the underpricing during the so-called "bubble period" of 1998-1999. Rather, they believed that specific rational explanations and agency conflicts would play a higher role in expounding this underpricing phenomenon, like the allocation of IPO shares and subsequent ownership of stocks.

Professors Along Brav and Paul Gompers (Brav & Gompers, 1997), on the other hand, had posited the contrasting evidence in their research. They had probed into the long-run underperformance of the IPOs after seperating the data into venture-backed and non-venture backed IPOs in the years 1975-1992. They had found that the venture-backed IPOs did perform better then the non-venture-backed IPOs when using equally-weighted returns. In their econometric tools employing comparable benchmarks and the Fama-French three-factor asset-pricing model, they had found that the smallest venture-backed IPOs did underperform, but the venture-backed IPOs in general, did not significantly underperform. As a matter of fact, underperformance in their non-venture backed sample was driven primarily by small issues, that is, those with market capitalization of less than $50 million.

Professors Barry, Muscarella, Peavy and Vetsuypens (Barry, Muscarella, Peavy & Vettsuypens, 1990), and Professors Megginson and Weiss (Megginson & Weiss, 1991) have found that stock markets react favorably to the presence of venture capital financing at the time of an IPO. Megginson and Weiss have also found that individuals, who are potentially more successful to fads and popular sentiments, hold a large fraction of shares after the IPO for nonventure-backed firms. Also, the fact is that venture capitalists stay on the board of directors long after the IPO issuance and may continue to provide access to capital that nonventure-backed IPOs lack. Professors Hoshi, Kashyap and Scharfstein (Hoshi, Kashyap & Scharfstein, 1991) have pointed out that because venture capitalists generally provide access to top-tier national investment and commercial bankers, they may partly overcome informational asymmetries that are essential with the start-up companies. Moreover, venture capitalists may have a hand in selecting the management team that help the firm perform better in the long run.

Recently, Professors Hellman and Puri (Hellman & Puri, 2002) have found that venture capital is related to a variety of professionalization measures, such as human resource policies, the adoption of stock option plans, and the hiring of a marketing VP. Venture-capital-backed companies are also more likely and faster to replace the founder with an outside CEO, both in situations that appear adversarial and those mutually agreed to. Their evidence also suggests that venture capitalists play roles over and beyond those of traditional financial intermediaries.

Finally, Professor Arvin Ghosh (Ghosh, 2003) has also found that, in general, returns of the venture-backed IPOs were higher than the nonventure-backed IPOs. Also, the first-day returns of these types of IPOs were higher than any other time periods, thus supporting the findings of others that IPOs in the United States had suffered from initial underpricing. He has also found that only the first-day closing price was significantly and negatively associated with most return variables. Both market capitalization and offer price as explanatory variables were significant only in a very limited number of regression equations, while the number of shares as the explanatory variables was not significant at all in most equations. Ghosh's results confirm the conclusion reached by Brav and Gompers that venture-backed IPOs performed better than the nonventure-backed IPOs during 1990-2000.

The following are the principal data sources for our study:

- The IPO Reporter
- Securities Data Company of Thomson Financial
- www.Ipo.com
- www.yahoo.com
- www.hoover.com
- Compustat Data File

Empirical Findings

In table 7.1, we have given the descriptive statistics regarding our sample of venture-backed and nonventure-backed Internet IPOs in the United States during 1996-2001. Although out of the total of 117 Internet IPOs, the number of venture-backed IPOs were 40 or 34.19 percent, the mean offer price of the venture-backed IPOs were higher than nonventure-backed IPOs, along with high standard deviation. Also, both the maximum value and the minimum value of the offer price were higher for the venture-backed IPOs than the nonventure-backed IPOs. However, both the number of shares offered and the value of market capitalization were higher for the nonventure-backed IPOs than the venture-backed IPOs. Also the mean and median value of the closing price of the nonventure-backed IPOs were higher than the venture-backed ones in our sample of the Internet IPOs in the United States during 1996-2001.

Table 7.1

Descriptive Statistics of the Venture-Backed and Nonventure-Backed Internet IPOs in the United States

A. Venture_backed Internet IPOs
(n= 40)

	Mean	Median	Stand. Dev.	Max. Value	Min. Value
Offer Price	$17.06	$15.00	10.90	$76.50	$7.00
Shares Offered (in Millions)	5.84	4.35	4.54	29.52	1.63
Market Cap. (in $mill.)	502.08	232.16	977.98	4,700.00	0.1994
First Day Closing Price	$31.43	$21.05	42.94	$265.01	$3.05

B. Nonventure-Backed Internet IPOs
(n= 77)

	Mean	Median	Stand. Dev.	Max. Value	Min. Value
Offer Price	$15.56	$14.02	6.56	$48.00	$5.13
Shares Offered (in Millions)	7.39	4.55	20.09	173.91	1.02
Market Cap. (in $mill)	1,582.08	1,232.08	802.11	56,740.00	0.2604
First Day Closing Price	$37.36	$22.86	42.88	$280.03	$4.50

In table 7.2, we have calculated the returns of different selected periods for the venture-backed Internet IPOs of our sample. Here we find that both the mean value and the median value of the first-day returns were much higher than the returns of other time periods, particularly as compared to the second-day and third-day returns which were drastically reduced. Both the six-month and one-year returns were negative for the venture-backed Internet IPOs. This also proves that the Internet IPOs were severely underpriced when the first-day closing price was compared with the offer price, as seen in many IPO studies of the United States.

Table 7.3 shows the returns of the nonventure-backed IPOs of different time periods of our sample. We find that the mean and the median value of the first-day return of this group were slightly higher than the returns of the venture-backed Internet IPOs. Also, both The second-day and third-day returns were precipitously lower as compared to the first-day return. But the six-month and one-year returns were positive and quite high as compared to the venture-backed Internet IPOs, as seen in table 7.2.

Table 7.2
Selected Returns of the Venture-Backed Internet IPOs (in Percentage)

	Mean	Median	Stand. Dev.	Max. Value	Min. Value
First Day Return	88.45	48.54	137.73	657.14	-48.53
Second Day Return	8.13	1.44	36.81	194.02	-34.09
Third Day Return	7.47	0.61	37.63	185.89	-40.11
First Month Return	19.32	1.21	70.93	267.00	-82.86
Six Month Return	-20.54	-33.01	52.24	92.83	-93.38
One Year Return	-32.06	-69.27	76.84	261.76	-98.42

Table 7.3
Selected Returns of the Nonventure-Backed Internet IPOs (in Percentage)

	Mean	Median	Stand. Dev	Max. Value	Min. Value
First Day Return	90.82	41.83	144.82	773.08	-50.00
Second Day Return	6.59	-0.25	29.99	149.33	-45.81
Third Day Return	4.20	-2.00	30.32	168.00	-43.67
First Month Return	26.13	8.44	65.42	244.26	-77.95
Six Month Return	59.57	12.60	156.29	713.22	-94.99
One Year Return	48.22	21.37	210.62	1271.00	-97.87

In table 7.4, we have calculated the operating ratios and the annual growth of cash flows of the venture-backed Internet IPOs. Except for 1997, both the mean and the median operating ratios were
positive during 1996-2001. It was highest in 1996 when the number
of Internet IPOs were very small, the second best year being 2000
when the number also started to dwindle. That was also the year
when the standard deviation of the mean operating ratio was the
highest. As for the annual growth of cash flows, the mean growth
rate was the highest in 2001 when the number of IPOs again became
much smaller, and the fluctuation of the mean ratio was also the
highest as reflected in its standard deviation. However, the negative
growth rate of cash flows in 1996 meant that the Internet sector had
just started to roll which had no time to build cash flows. Both the
high mean and median values in 1998-2000 showed the growth of
cash flows of the venture-backed IPOs in the United States.

Table 7.5 shows the mean and median operating ratios as well as
the mean and median growth of cash flows for the nonventure-backed
IPOs. Here we find that both the mean and median operating ratios
were positive throughout the time period covering 1996-2001, un-
like that of venture-backed IPOs. It was highest in 1997 when the
standard deviation was also the highest. The annual growth of cash

Table 7.4

Operating Ratio and Growth of Cash Flows of the Venture-Backed Internet IPOs

Year	Mean Operating Ratio	Median	Stand. Dev.	Annual Growth of Cash Flows	Median	Stand. Dev.
1996	18.58	7.94	26.05	-0.29	-2.23	3.28
1997	-21.37	-12.44	30.48	0.04	1.11	2.45
1998	11.02	0.78	22.91	5.09	3.42	6.33
1999	7.69	0.96	17.85	5.48	2.85	8.93
2000	16.86	1.78	40.13	6.42	2.51	9.72
2001	4.36	1.13	9.99	9.03	7.93	12.00

Table 7.5

Operating Ratio and Growth of Cash Flows of the Nonventure-Backed Internet IPOs

Year	Mean Operating Ratio	Median	Stand. Dev.	Annual Growth of Cash Flows	Median	Stand. Dev.
1996	1.46	1.43	0.48	1.17	1.26	0.42
1997	34.76	3.86	82.51	18.87	4.22	27.33
1998	15.07	1.33	33.97	15.18	6.55	23.03
1999	13.14	1.52	37.89	15.20	3.88	32.44
2000	8.27	1.25	45.44	18.73	3.06	58.59
2001	6.60	1.11	30.76	17.19	3.18	47.27

flows was also the highest in 1997, the second best result coming in 2000. The very high rate of growth of cash flows again reflects the robustness of this sector among the IPOs. When we compare the results with that of table 7.4, we find that the annual growth of cash flows was much higher for the nonventure-backed IPOs than that of the venture-backed IPOs during 1996-2001—the period covered by our study.

We have also employed the OLS regression model in order to explore the causal relationship between the IPO return as the dependent variable, and various relevant variables as the independent variables, for both the data-sets of venture-backed IPOs and the nonventure-backed Internet IPOs. The multiple regression equation is of the form:

$$AR = a_0 + b_1 \, FC + b_2 \, OP + b_3 \, SO + b_4 \, MC$$

Where:

AR = Returns of different periods;

FC = First-day closing price ($);

OP = Offer Price;

SO = Shares offered (million);

MC = Market capitalization ($ million).

In table 7.6, we have shown the regression returns for the venture-backed Internet IPOs listed in both the NYSE and NASDAQ stock markets. We find that only the first-day closing price (FC) was significantly and negatively associated with the return variables in four of the six equations, particularly for the first two days as well as for the six-month and one-year returns. Offer Price (OP) was significant in two out of the six equations, but the sign was negative and consistent for all the equations. Shares Offered (SO) was significant

Table 7.6
Multiple Regression Equations of Returns as the Dependent Variable
(Venture-Backed IPOs)

Dependent Variable (ARs)	Independent Variables				R^2	F-Ratio
	FC	OP	SO	MC		
First-Day Return (AR1)	-2.557*	-0.432	0.816	0.024	0.650	6.281
	(-7.254)	(-0.331)	(0.268)	(0.731)		
Second-Day Return (AR2)	-1.028*	-0.656	0.461	0.004	0.556	4.528
	(-1.919)	(1.147)	(0.345)	(0.719)		
Third-Day Return (AR3)	-0.939	-0.725**	0.565	0.008	0.303	4.001
	(-0.397)	(-1.358)	(0.424)	(1.028)		
First-Month Return (AR4)	-0.144	-0.998*	0.738	0.013	0.367	5.632
	(-0.157)	(1.911)	(0.288)	(1.065)		
Six-Month Return (AR5)	-0.118*	-0.626	0.726	0.018	0.257	4.638
	(-1.818)	(-0.816)	(0.405)	(0.259)		
One-Year Return (AR6)	-0.115*	-1.044	-0.264*	0.080*	0.276	3.251
	(-2.421)	(-0.996)	(-1.797)	(2.675)		

t-values of the independent variables are in parenthesis.
*1 % level of significance.
**5 % level of significance.

Table 7.7
Multiple Regression Equations of Returns as the Dependent Variable
(Nonventure-Backed IPOs)

Dependent Variable (Ars)	Independent Variables				R^2	F-Ratio
	FC	OP	SO	MC		
First-Day Return (AR1)	-2.996*	-2.492*	-0.701**	-0.008	0.432	6.472
	(-6.229)	(-1.619)	(1.158)	(-0.492)		
Second-Day Return (AR2)	-0.661*	-0.630	-0.073	0.001	0.351	6.031
	(-1.558)	(-0.921)	(-0.482)	(0.557)		
Third-Day Return (AR3)	0.078	-0.921*	-0.036	0.002	0.342	5.370
	(0.696)	(-1.421)	(-0.250)	(0.403)		
First-Month Return (AR4)	0.085	-1.346	-1.191	0.002	0.286	7.704
	(0.282)	(0.817)	(0.522)	(1.083)		
Six-Month Return (AR5)	-0.281*	-2.792*	-0.789	0.010	0.324	6.648
	(-1.480)	(2.301)	(-1.046)	(0.857)		
One-Year Return (AR6)	-0.378*	-3.513*	-1.013	0.013*	0.485	4.110
	(-2.436)	(-2.701)	(-0.906)	(1.433)		

t-values of the independent variables are in parenthesis.
*1 % level of significance.
**5 % level of significance.

only for the one-year return, as was Market Capitalization (MC). Thus the significance of the FC variable indicates the underpricing of the IPOs, particularly on the first day, when the IPOs were offered to the public for the first time.

Table 7.7 shows the regression results for the nonventure-backed Internet IPOs, also listed in the NYSE and the NASDAQ market. Here we also find that the first-day closing price (FC) was negatively and significantly associated with the return variables in four out of six equations, also for the same crucial time periods as in table 7.6. Offer Price (OP) was also significantly and negatively associated with four out of six equations. But Shares Offered (SO) was significantly (and negatively) associated only with the first-day return as the dependent variable, as Market Capitalization (MC) was significant (positive) only for the one-year return. Both the R^2 and F-ratio indicate the relevancy of the equations, following the methodology of the OLS regression model.

In table 7.8, we have combined the data for both the venture-backed and nonventure-backed IPOs in the NYSE and NASDAQ stock market. Here we find that the First-day closing Price (FC) was significantly and negatively associated with the return variables in three out of the six equations, again for the crucial time periods of the IPO issuance. But Offer Price (OP) was significantly and negatively associated with the return variables in *all* of the six equations, not seen in tables 7.6 and 7.7. Shares Offered (SO), however, was significant (negatively) only with the first-day return, as was Market Capitalization (MC). Again, the relatively decent values of R^2 and high F-ratios indicate the statistical relevancy of the equations.

Concluding Remarks

We have thus found that the first-day returns were much higher than any other time periods for both the venture-backed and nonventure-backed Internet IPOs, although the returns of the latter group was slightly higher than the former group. Also, the annual growth of cash flows was much higher for the nonventure-backed Internet IPOs than the venture-backed Internet IPOs. As for the regression results, only the first-day closing price was significantly and negatively associated with all the return variables.

Table 7.8
Multiple Regression Equation of Returns as the Dependent Variable
(Combined Data)

Dependent Variable (Ars)	Independent Variables				R^2	F-Ratio
	FC	OP	SO	MC		
First-Day Return (AR1)	-2.632*	-1.604*	-0.679**	-0.106*	0.477	6.455
	(-3.502)	(1.302)	(-1.406)	(-3.564)		
Second-Day Return (AR2)	-0.346	-0.610**	-0.065	0.002	0.357	5.238
	(-0.571)	(-1.586)	(-0.387)	(0.631)		
Third-Day Return (AR3)	0.057	-0.786*	-0.030	0.003	0.315	7.704
	(0.719)	(-2.082)	(-0.182)	(0.349)		
First-Month Return (AR4)	0.021	-1.131**	-0.165**	0.002	0.471	4.133
	(0.116)	(-1.348)	(0.447)	(0.216)		
Six-Month Return (AR5)	-0.136**	-3.207*	-0.624	0.012	0.457	6.277
	(-1.433)	(-2.161)	(-0.951)	(0.702)		
One-Year Return (AR6)	-0.302*	-2.468*	-0.947	0.013	0.465	6.314
	(-2.644)	(1.966)	(-1.003)	(0.448)		

t-values of the independent variables are in parenthesis.

*1 % level of significance.

**5 % level of significance.

References

Barry, C., C. Muscarella, J. Peavy & M. Vetsuypens (1990). The role of venture capital in the creation of public companies: evidence from the going-public process. *Journal of Financial Economics*, 27, 447-476.

Brav, A. & P.A. Gompers (1997). Myth or reality? The long-run underperformance of initial public offerings: evidence from venture and nonventure capital-based companies. *Journal of Finance*, 52, 1791-1821.

Fama, E & K. French (1993). Common risk factors in the returns of stocks and bonds. *Journal of Financial Economics*, 33, 3-55.

Ghosh, A. (2003). Pricing and long-run performance of the venture-backed and nonventure-backed IPOs. *International Business & Economic Research Journal*, 2, 87-93.

Hellman, T. & M. Puri (2002). Venture capital and the performance of start-up firms: empirical evidence. *Journal of Finance*, 58, 169-197.

Hoshi, T., A. Kashyap & D. Scharfstein (1991). Corporate structure, liquidity, and investment. *Quarterly Journal of Economics*, 106, 33-60.

Megginson, W. & K. Weiss (1991). Venture capitalist certification in initial public offerings. *Journal of Finance*, 46, 879-903.

Ritter, J. R. (1991). The long-run performance of initial public offerings. *Journal of Finance*, 46, 3-27.

Ritter, J. R. & I. Welch (2002). A review of IPO activity, pricing, and allocations. *Journal of Finance*, 57, 1795-1828.

8

Gross Spread of the Underwriters and Offer Price of the IPOs, 1990-2000*

Initial Public Offerings (IPOs) were one of the principal engines that fueled the economic expansion of the 1990s in the United States. Thousands of them were issued during the last decade and hardly a week went by when a few of the IPOs were not issued, particularly in the high-technology sector. Along with the general IPOs, the role of Internet IPOs was also significant which caused the stock market "bubble" in 1998-1999 that collapsed in early 2000. It was quite possible that without the IPOs, the stock market boom of the last decade would not have been sustained for such a long time and with such vigor as to push the U.S. stock prices to a historic high.

The pricing process in an IPO is conducted through the collaborative arrangement of the issuing firm, its lead underwriter and the prospective investors. One of the most crucial tasks of the issuing firm is to select the lead underwriter which is usually an investment bank. Selection of the underwriter depends on the investment bank's reputation, expertise and quality of research in the industry where the firm competes. The lead underwriter becomes the book-running manager who forms the syndicate and is responsible for the whole IPO process. The initial agreement between the underwriter and the issuing company is called the "Letter of Intent" and it protects the underwriter against any uncovered expenses in the event that the offer is withdrawn. The Letter of Intent remains valid until the underwriting agreement is executed at the time of pricing the shares.

In the IPO market, the offer price of the new stocks is mainly determined by the underwriters. The pricing of an IPO is a delicate

---

*This chapter was written jointly with my Colleague Professor Carol Boyer at William Paterson University of New Jersey. The errors, of course, are mine.

balancing act. The lead underwriter has to worry about two different sets of clients—the company going public that wants to raise as much capital as possible, and the investors buying the shares who expect to see some immediate appreciation on their investment. The lead underwriter usually tries to price a deal so that the opening day price appreciation is about 15 percent. Of course, many hot Internet IPOs showed above-average increases on the first day of being publicly traded. Once the offer price has been agreed upon by the issuing company and the lead underwriter—and at least two days after the potential investors receive the final prospectus—an IPO is declared effective. This is usually done after the stock market closes, with trading in the new stock starting the next day. Thus the lead underwriter is primarily responsible for ensuing smooth trading in a company's stock during those first few crucial days of public trading of the IPOs.

Literature Review

In their celebrated article called "The Seven Percent Solution," Professors Hsuan-Chi Chen and Jay R. Ritter (Chen & Ritter, 2000) examined the commissions paid to the investment bankers, known as the gross spreads or underwriting discounts, of 1,111 IPOs raising capital amounts between $20 and $80 million in the United States during 1995-1998. They found that more than 90 percent of the issuers paid gross spreads of exactly 7 percent. This clustering of spreads of exactly 7 percent was not as widespread during 1985-1987, when only about one-quarter of moderate sized IPOs had spreads of exactly 7 percent. Chen and Ritter also found that spreads on IPOs outside of the United States, such as in Australia, Japan, Hong Kong or Europe, are approximately half the level of those in the United States. Furthermore, spreads within the United States for bonds, convertible bonds and seasoned equity offerings do not show this clustering around 7 percent. They argue that several features of the IPO underwriting market such as analyst coverage and buy recommendations, and the perceived importance of underwriter prestige, facilitate these high spreads. Chen and Ritter suspect implicit collusion or "strategic pricing" for their pattern of 7 percent spread among the investment bankers.

Professor Robert Hansen (Hansen, 2002) has also examined recently of this phenomenon of "7 percent contract" by the investment bankers in the United States. He has tested two competing hypotheses, that either investment bankers collude to profit from their 7 percent spread, or it is the standardized form of commitment contract that better suits the IPO market. In general, the tests conducted by Hansen do not reveal any evidence of collusion. The IPO market is unconcentrated, entry into the market has been rather free, and 7 percent commission does not contain abnormal profits relative to other IPOs. Hansen has pointed out that the 7 percent contract has persisted in the midst of the U.S. Department of Justice investigation of collusion allegations concludes strongly against collusion.

Professor Hansen has discussed three possible advantages for the 7 percent contract in serving IPOs. The first advantage is that a 7 percent spread may narrow informational externalities created by the large ex ante error in valuing speculative IPO firms. A spread's gap from what was expected could raise suspicions about firm value and underwriter veracity, and a uniform spread across IPOs may limit doubt about what underwriter compensation is going to be. The second advantage is the reduced moral hazard. The verifiability of underwriter placement effort is impaired by a large IPO valuation. A flat spread provides a simple ex ante delegated monitoring mechanism that encourages search, thus raising value. The third possible advantage of a fixed spread is lowering contracting cost. In the case of IPOs, the negotiations are complicated by the uncertainty about the market price of the firm's stock. The 7 percent contract helps simplify the complex contracting environment by reducing the number of items to negotiate and the ensuing haggling.

Professors Ellis, Michaely and O'Hraira (Ellis, et. al., 2000) have examined the aftermarket trading of underwriters in the three-month period after an IPO is issued. They have found that the lead underwriter is always the dominant market maker. The lead underwriter takes substantial inventory position in the after market trading, and co-managers play a negligible role in aftermarket trading. The lead underwriter engages in stabilization activity for less successful IPOs, and uses overallotment option to reduce the inventory risk. On analyzing the inventory position and trading profits of the underwriters, Ellis, et al., have found that the market making activity is a standalone profit center. They have also found that trading profits increase as the issue is more underpriced. They have found positive relationships among trading profits and size and turnover of the IPOs. Overall, making markets in the first three months after the IPO accounts for less than 23 percent of the lead underwriter's compensation, the remaining 77 percent of compensation comes from the underwriting fees.

Aggarwal (Aggarwal, 2000) found that the insider stabilizing activities by the underwriters are less transparent to investors or researchers. The study analyzed three types of aftermarket activities of the underwriters: pure stabilization, short covering, and penalty bids. One of the major findings is that pure stabilization does not occur—underwriters do not post "stabilizing bids" to provide price support. But aftermarket short covering does occur to stimulate demand, and penalty bids to restrict supply by penalizing the flipping of shares. The study finds that in more than half of the IPOs sampled, a short position of an average 10.75 percent of shares offered in twenty-two transactions over 16.6 days in the aftermarket, resulting in a loss of 3.61 percent of underwriting fees. But the underwriters manage the stabilization process and limit their losses by using a combination of short covering in the aftermarket, penalty bids, and exercise of overallotment option.

Empirical Findings

In table 8.1, we have shown the gross spread of the underwriters of the United States IPOs in both the New York Stock Exchange (NYSE) and NASDAQ markets covering 1990-1999. Here we find that, contrary to the findings of many others, the gross spread of the U.S. underwriters was never exactly 7 percent of the money raised by the IPOs. It was nearly close to that only in 1999 for the NYSE stocks, and slightly above that in 1990, but was different for the other years covered. The gross spread was as high as 9.36 percent in

Table 8.1
Underwriting Gross Spread for IPOs in the United States, 1990-1999

	NYSE	NASDAQ	Internet	Average
1990	7.12	8.18	.	7.65
1991	6.83	7.69	.	7.26
1992	9.36	10.37	.	9.87
1993	7.92	11.06	.	9.49
1994	6.76	8.11	7.00	7.29
1995	5.73	10.27	7.98	7.99
1996	9.79	8.72	10.52	9.68
1997	8.22	7.94	9.86	8.67
1998	8.82	8.73	7.40	8.32
1999	6.96	7.24	6.84	7.01
Avg.	6.97	8.83	8.26	8.32

Source: SDC/Thomson Financial

1992 and was as low as 5.73 percent in 1995 for the IPOs listed in the NYSE. Thus the average gross spread was not 7 percent at all for the U.S. underwriters. "The 7 Percent Solution," as dramatically stated by Chen and Ritter, might be true for their sample firms, but not true when the whole population was taken into account.

This was also true for the IPOs listed in the NASDAQ, and separately for its Internet stocks sub-sample, except in 1994 for the latter group. For the NASDAQ IPOs, the average gross spread was as high as 11.06 percent, but was never below 7 percent, averaging 8.83 percent for the ten-year period. The Internet stocks appeared in the IPO market from 1994 when the gross spread was exactly 7 percent, then went up to 10.52 percent in 1996, coming down to below 7 percent in 1999. The average gross spread of the underwriters for the Internet stocks was 8.27 percent during 1996-1999, and the average gross spread for both markets was 8.32 percent during 1990-1999.

In table 8.2, we have given the proceeds and the market shares of ten leading underwriters during 1998-2000—the heyday of the United States IPOs. Here we find that Goldman Sachs had emerged as the leader in market share in both 1999 and 2000, from its third place in 1998, while Morgan Stanley Dean Witter fell to second from the top position in 1998. Merrill Lynch fell further down to the fifth position in both 1999 and 2000 from the second position in 1998. Credit Suisse First Boston (CSFB) had moved one notch up to the third position in both 1999 and 2000 from its fourth position in 1998, while Salomon Smith Barney went one position down in 1999 and 2000 from its third position in 1998. It is interesting to note however, that China International Capital found a place on this lofty list in 2000, while Donaldson, Lufkin and Jenrette lost its separate identity, and became a part of CSFB in 2000.

Table 8.3 shows the offer price in both the NYSE and NASDAQ markets along with the Internet IPOs during 1990-1999. We find that the average offer price in the NYSE was quite high during the yearly years of the 1990s—reaching as high as $73.75 in 1992, and falling to a low of $18.72 in 1996, and then again, rising to $73.51 in 1999. During the "bubble year" of the IPO stocks in 1999, the offer price fell to $27.33—a 63 percent decline in one year. The average offer price of the NYSE for the whole decade however, was $49.22.

As for the NASDAQ stock market, the average offer price of the IPOs was much lower than the NYSE market, being lowest in 1999 when the economy was still suffering from a shallow recession, and

Table 8.2
Ten Leading Underwriters in Initial Public Offerings

Manager	2000		1999		1998	
	Proceeds (in billion)	Market Share	Proceeds (in billion)	Market Share	Proceeds (in billion)	Market Share
Goldman Sachs	$17.7	24.2%	$12.9	20.3%	$3.42	9.3%
Morgan Stanley Dean Witter	11.3	15.5	12.8	20.2	7.85	21.3
Credit Suisse First Boston	11.2	15.3	9.8	15.4	1.90	5.2
Salomon Smith Barney	8.9	12.1	2.5	4.0	2.47	6.7
Merrill Lynch	6.7	9.2	7.4	11.6	7.11	19.3
Deutsche Bank	3.1	4.2	2.1	3.3	1.26	3.4
J. P. Morgan	2.6	3.5	2.1	3.3	0.98	2.7
Lehman Brothers	2.5	3.4	2.9	4.5	0.79	2.2
Fleet Boston Financial	2.1	2.9	2.7	4.2	0.59	1.6
China International Capital (D.L.J. in 1998)	1.3	1.8	...	...	1.21	3.3
Top 10 Totals	67.4	92.1	57.3	90.1	27.6	74.9
Industry Totals	73.3	100.0	63.5	100.0	36.8	100.0

Source: Wall Street Journal, Year-end Review, covering 1998-2000.

Table 8.3
Offer Price for IPOs in the United States, 1990-1999

	NYSE	NASDAQ	Internet	Average
1990	57.82	9.30	.	33.56
1991	62.61	16.02	.	39.32
1992	73.75	30.87	.	52.31
1993	45.17	17.04	.	31.11
1994	45.01	12.52	12.25	23.26
1995	55.65	18.24	10.57	46.70
1996	18.72	16.94	12.42	16.03
1997	32.67	22.05	16.91	23.88
1998	73.51	24.44	23.00	40.32
1999	27.33	14.55	23.56	21.81
Avg.	49.22	18.19	16.45	32.83

Source: SDC/Thomson Financial

was highest in 1998—the so-called 'bubble period' of the IPO issuance. The average offer price for the whole period (1990-1999) for this market was only $18.20. For the Internet stocks the average offer price was highest in 1999—the "Year of the Internet"—and lowest in 1995 when this market was just getting started. The average offer price for the Internet IPOs in our sample was only $16.45—lower than even that of the NASDAQ market and 67 percent lower as compared to the NYSE market. The average offer price of the IPOs for all the markets combined and for the whole decade, was, however, $3.83—the reason being that the offer price of the NYSE had raised it at a much higher level as compared to the average of the two markets.

Table 8.4 shows data on the filing range and actual IPO prices during 1980-1999, dividing into three sub-periods. The data indicates that the high price of filing price range had declined considerably from 1980-1989 to 1990-1994 and 1995-1999, while the low price dipped slightly during the same periods. But the primary shares filed as a percentage of primary shares offered was more than halved in the later two sub-periods as compared to 1980-1989. In the case of issues priced above the filing range, it more than tripled in 1995-1999 from 1980-1989, while the issues priced within the filing range, which was more than 75 percent in 1980-1989, fell by only 4 percentage points in 1995-1999 as compared to 1980-1989.

Table 8.5 shows that the underwriter fees as percentage of the principal amount raised had remained virtually unchanged from

Table 8.4
Prices and Issues in Filing Range, 1980-1999

	A. Price in Filing Range		
	1980-1989	1990-1994	1995-1999
High Price of Filing Price Range	$31.17	$14.29	$12.74
Low Price of Filing Price Range	13.38	13.46	11.05
Primary Shares Filed As % of Primary Shares Offered	77.59	32.48	31.57
	B. Issues in Filing Range		
Issue Priced Above Filing Range	5.78%	7.79%	16.91%
Issue Priced Within Filing Range	75.27	76.17	71.10
Issue Priced Below Price Range	18.93	14.04	12.03

Source: SDC/ Thomson Financial.

Table 8.5
Underwriter Fees, Insider Shares, and Shares in Lock-Up

Years	Underwriter Fees As % of Principal Amount	Reallowance Fees As % of Principal Amount	Percentage of Insider Shares Before After	Percentage of Shares in Lock-up
1970-1979	1.789	2.300	15.31 30.98	NA
1980-1989	1.712	1.774	17.55 55.00	69.39
1990-1999	1.592	1.029	65.14 43.59	89.19
1990-1994	1.622	1.121	64.31 41.18	81.92
1995-1999	1.572	0.961	65.70 45.22	96.57

Source: SDC/ Thomson Financial.

1970-1979 to 1980-1989, and dipped slightly during 1990-1999. But the reallowance fees as a percentage of the principal amount had fallen considerably from 2.300 percent in 1970-1979 to 1.029 percent in 1990-1999—a 55 percent decline during the entire time period. As for the percentage of insider shares before and after the companies went public, it had more than doubled between 1970-1979, but decreased substantially during 1980-1989 and 1990-1999. But the percentage of shares in lock-up by the management and venture capitalists had increased dramatically from 69.35 percent in 1980-1989 to 89.19 percent in 1990-1999. When we break down the recent decade into two sub-periods, the percentage of shares in lock-up was almost doubled during 1990-1994, and was more than 96 percent during 1995-1999.

In table 8.6, we have employed the multiple regression equations with gross spread as the dependent variable, and fifteen relevant variables as the independent variables for IPOs in both the stock markets. We find that, for the IPOs listed in the NYSE, both the common equity and debt/equity ratio were positively associated with the gross spread of the underwriters where the t-values were significant at the 1 percent level. But the days in lock-up was negatively associated with the gross spread where the t-value was significant at the 5 percent level. However, all the three variables were associated with only a small variation in gross spread, amounting to less than 1 percent.

For the multiple regression equations of the NASDAQ IPOs, ROA was negatively associated with the gross spread, while the offer price was negatively associated with the gross spread—the t-values being significant at the 1 percent level. As for the Internet IPOs, unfortunately, none of the independent variables was significant with the gross spread where the F-ratio was also not significant at any level. However, the high R^2 of the multiple regression equations for the

Table 8.6
Multiple Regression with Gross Spread as the Dependent Variable.

Gross Spread $_{i,t} = b_0 + b_1$ Book Value$_{i,t} + b_2$ Common Equity$_{i,t} + b_3$ EBIT$_{i,t} + b_4$ Debt/ Equity$_{i,t} + b_5$ Market Value$_{i,t} + b_6$ ROA$_{i,t} + b_7$ ROE$_{i,t} + b_8$ Capitalization$_{i,t} + b_9$ Total Debt$_{i,t} + b_{10}$ Revenue$_{i,t} + b_{11}$ Percent of Insider Shares$_{i,t} + b_{12}$ Price$_{i,t} + b_{13}$ Net Income After Tax $_{i,t} + b_{14}$ Days in Lock-Up$_{i,t} + b_{15}$ Number of Employees$_{i,t} + e_{i,t}$

	NYSE		NASDAQ		Internet	
INTERCEPT	7.197	(8.340)	8.111	(29.268)	9.188	(14.308)
BV	-0.083	(-1.043)	0.028	(0.476)	-0.037	(-0.612)
CE	0.024	(2.104)**	0.002	(0.374)	-0.024	(-0.885)
EBIT	-0.058	(-1.154)	-0.011	(-0.446)	0.003	(0.225)
DE	0.004	(3.613)**	0.000	(0.329)	-0.001	(-0.400)
MVA	-0.001	(-0.396)	0.000	(0.519)	-0.001	(-0.587)
ROA	-0.025	(-0.916)	0.027	(2.907)**		
ROE	0.026	(1.089)	0.001	(0.583)		
CAP	-0.010	(-1.065)	0.001	(0.205)	0.025	(0.835)
TDEBT	0.010	(0.962)	0.003	(0.774)	-0.024	(-0.821)
REV	-0.001	(-0.488)	-0.001	(-0.172)	-0.011	(-0.882)
INSIDER	0.004	(0.677)	0.001	(0.416)	-0.012	(-1.156)
PRICE	0.008	(0.915)	-0.094	(-3.401)**	-0.072	(-1.313)
NIAT	0.009	(0.131)	-0.060	(-1.183)	-0.015	(-0.504)
LUP	-0.002	(-1.883)*	-0.001	(-1.335)		
EMP	-0.001	(-0.816)				
R-square	0.8132		0.3260		0.3378	
Adj R-sq	0.6121		0.2207		0.0950	
F	1.391		4.043**		3.095**	
N	288		4227		114	

**, * Significantly different from zero at the 1 % and 5 % level, respectively.
(t-statistics for the individual parameters are in parentheses)

NYSE IPOs indicate the robustness of the association of the three independent variables with gross spread of the underwriters.

In table 8.7, we have fitted the multiple regression equations with offer price as the dependent variable, and almost the same fifteen independent variables used in table 8.6 for the two stock markets. Here we find that the common equity was negatively and significantly associated with the dependent variable in the NYSE IPO market. Both the market capitalization and revenue variables were positively associated with the offer price, while total debt was negatively associated with the offer price. In all these four equations, the t-values were significant at the 1 percent level.

Table 8.7
Multiple Regression with Offer Price as the Dependent Variable.

Gross Spread $_{i,t}$ = b_0 + b_1 Book Value$_{i,t}$ + b_2 Common Equity$_{i,t}$ + b_3 EBIT$_{i,t}$ + b_4 Debt/Equity$_{i,t}$ + b_5 Market Value$_{i,t}$ + b_6 ROA$_{i,t}$ + b_7 ROE$_{i,t}$ + b_8 Capitalization$_{i,t}$ + b_9 Total Debt$_{i,t}$ + b_{10} Revenue$_{i,t}$ + b_{11} Percent of Insider Shares$_{i,t}$ + b_{12} Price$_{i,t}$ + b_{13} Net Income After Tax $_{i,t}$ + b_{14} Days in Lock-Up$_{i,t}$ + b_{15} Number of Employees$_{i,t}$ + $e_{i,t}$

	NYSE		NASDAQ		Internet	
INTERCEPT	-42.412	(-0.691)	13.669	(5.070)	12.271	(2.306)
BV	0.446	(0.188)	1.034	(5.879)**	0.479	(2.655)**
CE	-0.917	(-3.106)**	-0.017	(-0.891)	0.012	(0.140)
EBIT	1.071	(0.711)	-0.072	(-0.791)	0.093	(1.772)*
DE	-0.031	(-0.687)	0.001	(0.591)	-0.002	(-0.675)
MVA	0.020	(0.567)	0.027	(8.761)**	0.017	(3.166)**
ROA	0.945	(1.231)	0.078	(2.380)**		
ROE	-0.542	(-0.761)	0.010	(1.662)*		
CAP	0.768	(3.533)**	-0.001	(-0.334)	-0.041	(-0.424)
TDEBT	-0.865	(-3.613)**	-0.015	(-0.982)	0.048	(0.499)
REV	0.121	(4.236)**	0.003	(0.875)	-0.008	(-0.202)
INSIDER	-0.184	(-0.983)	0.008	(1.656)*	0.008	(0.240)
GS	7.060	(0.915)	-1.140	(-3.401)**	-0.749	(-1.313)
NIAT	-1.993	(-0.982)	-0.294	(-1.681)*	-0.204	(-2.294)**
LUP	0.049	(1.115)	-0.011	(-3.549)**		
EMP			0.001	(0.379)		
R-squared	0.8906		0.6962		0.7743	
Adj R-squared	0.7727		0.6488		0.6916	
F	7.557**		14.669**		9.357**	
N	288		4227		114	

**, * Significantly different from zero at the 1 % and 5 % level, respectively.
(t-statistics for the individual parameters are in parentheses)

But when we look into the NASDAQ IPO market, the book value, the market value, the return on assets and the return on equity were positively and significantly associated with the offer price, while the gross spread, NIAT, and days in lock-up were negatively associated with the offer price. The percent of insider shares variable, however, was positively associated with the offer price where the t-value was significant at the 5 percent level. For the Internet IPOs, table 8.7 shows that the book value (BV), EBIT, and market value of assets were positively associated with the offer price, while NIAT was negatively associated with the offer price. Both the high R^2 and the F-ratio in all these markets indicate the good fit and the robustness of the regression equations.

Conclusion

Thus the average gross spread of the United States underwriters for the IPOs during 1990-1999 was not exactly 7 percent. It moved with a range of 5.73 percent to 11.06 percent when both the NYSE and the NASDAQ markets were combined. The average offer price also flucturated within the wide range of $9.30 to $73, 75 percent for the two markets combined. But the high price range fell quite a bit during 1995-1999, as the low price range fell slightly during the same period. The same was true for the underwriters' fees as percentage of principal amount. The multiple regression equations indicate that gross spread as the dependent variable was negatively and significantly associated with common equity and days in lockup in the NYSE, and with ROA and the offer price for the NASDAQ market.

References

Aggarwal, R., 2000, "Stabilization Activities by Underwriters after Initial Public Offerings," *Journal of Finance*, 55, 1075-1103.

Ang, J., and S. Zhang, 2002, "Underwriting Relationship: Initial Setup Costs, Underwriting Fees, And First Move Advantage," *Working Paper*, Florida State University.

Benveniste, L., and P. Spindt, 1989, "How Investment Bankers determine the Offer Price and Allocation of New Issues," *Journal of Financial Economics*, 24, 343-362.

Chen, H-C., and J. R. Ritter, 2000, "The Seven Percent Solution," *Journal of Finance*, 55, 1105-1131.

Carter, R., and S. Manaster, 1990, "Initial Public Offerings and Underwriter Reputation," *Journal of Finance*, 45, 1045-1067.

Ellis, K. R., R. Michaely, and M. O'Hara, 2000, "When the Underwriter is the Market Maker: An Examination of Trading in the IPO Aftermarket," *Journal of Finance*, 55, 1039-1074.

9

Accuracy of Analysts' IPO
Earnings Forecasts*

Making investment decisions regarding IPO are extremely challenging. In recent times, individual investors are actively trading in the stock market using the proprietary and non-proprietary information about the firm. Corporate earnings forecasts are an important investment tool for investors. Corporate earnings forecast come from two sources: financial analysts and the firm's management. As an insider, the management has advantage of possessing more information, and hence provides a more accurate earnings forecast. However, because of the existing relationship of the company with its key investor group, the management may have a tendency to take an optimistic view and overestimate its future earnings. In contrast, the financial analysts are less informed about the company and often rely on management briefings. They have more experiences in the overall market and economics, and are expected to analyze companies with more objectivity. Hence, analysts should provide reliable and more accurate earnings forecast.

The objective of this chapter is to study the accuracy of the corporate earnings forecasts made by the financial analysts at the time of an IPO. At the time of an IPO, especially during the nineties, investors had very limited information about the past performance of the firm and had to rely on the accuracy of the earnings forecasts and the resulting valuation. During the past two decades, considerable research has been done on the accuracy of the earnings forecasts and its determinants. However, to the best of our knowledge,

* This chapter was written jointly with my colleague Professor J.K. Yun at William Paterson University of New Jersey, and with Professors Richard Cohen and Suresh Srivastava of the University of Alaska Anchorage. The errors, of course, are mine.

none of those studies have focused on the accuracy of the earnings forecasts following an IPO. This research is an attempt to bridge that knowledge gap.

Literature Review

There are vast amounts of past research available on the relative accuracy, bias and determinants of forecast accuracy. Here we will review only a few of those articles (omission of an article is not a reflection on its merit or its contribution to the literature). Jaggi (1980) examined the impact of company size on forecast accuracy using management's earnings from the *Wall Street Journal*, and analysts' earnings forecast from Value Line Investment Survey from 1971 to 1974. He argued that because a large firm has strong financial and human capital resources, its management's earnings forecast would be more accurate than analyst's. The sample data were classified into six categories based on size of the firm's total revenue to examine the factors that attribute to the accuracy of management's earnings forecast with analysts. The result of his research did not support his hypothesis that management's forecast is more accurate—than analyst's.

Bhushan (1989) assumed that it is more profitable to trade large company's stock because large companies have better liquidity than small ones. Therefore, the availability of information is related to company size. His research supported his hypothesis that larger the company size, the more information is available to financial analysts and the more accurate their earnings forecasts are.

Kross, Ro, and Schreoder (1990) proposed that brokerage firm's characteristics influence analysts' earnings forecasting accuracy. In their analysis, sample analysts' earnings forecasts from 1980 to 1981 were obtained from the *Value Line Investment Survey*, and the market value of a firm is used as the size of the firm. The results of this study on analysts' earnings forecasts did not find a positive relation between the company size and the analyst's forecast accuracy.

Bartley and Cameron (1991) examined the determinants associated with the relative accuracy of earnings by managers and by financial analysts. Sample data of management's earnings forecasts from the year 1975 to 1979 are extracted from the *Wall Street Journal Index*, and analyst' earnings were the mean earnings forecasts from the *Standard & Poor's* Earings Forecaster. They found that management's forecast accuracy is superior to prior analyst's forecast, and that there is no significant difference between managers' and posterior analyst's forecast.

Higgins (1998) examined the relationship between the level of management's earnings forecast disclosure and the relative precision of analyst's earnings forecast using selected samples from 11,000 companies of seven different countries covering the period from 1991 to 1995. The disclosure level of management's earnings forecast were set as the independent variables in his analysis, and analyst's earnings forecast was used as the dependent variable in regression model to examine such relationship. His findings were: the higher the country's requirements in disclosing company's earnings forecast, the more accurate was the analyst's earnings forecast and the lower the optimistic error was. But with a less regulated policy on management's earnings forecast disclosure, analysts' earnings forecast has lower degree of accuracy and higher level of optimistic error.

Das, Levine and Sivaramakrishnan (1998) used a cross-sectional approach to study the optimistic behavior of financial analysis. Especially, they focused on the predictive accuracy of past information of analysts' earnings forecast associated with the magnitude of the bias in analysts' earnings forecasts. The sample selection covers the time period from the 1989 to 1993 with 274 companies' earnings forecasts information. A regression method was used in this research. The term "optimistic behavior" is referred to as the optimistic earnings forecast made by financial analysts. The authors hypothesized the following scenario: there is higher demand for non-public information for firms whose earnings are more difficult to predict than for firms whose earnings can be accurately forecasted using public information. Their finding supports the hypothesis that analysts will make more optimistic forecasts for low predictability firms with an assumption that optimistic forecasts facilitates access to management's non-public information.

Orie, Kile and O'Kcelo (1999) examine the predictive value of management discussion and analysis (MD&A) information. More specifically, it tests the association between properties of analysts' earnings forecasts and MD&A quality, where the SEC measures MD&A quality. It is found that high MD&A ratings are associated with less error and less dispersion in analysts' earnings forecasts after controlling for many other expected influences on analysts' forecasts. It is also found that the estimated regression coefficients are consistent with MD&A information having a substantial effect on earnings forecasts.

Clement (1999) studied the relationship between the analysts' quality and their forecast accuracy. Using the *I/B/E/S* database, the author has found that earnings forecast accuracy is positively related with an analyst's experience and employer size, and inversely related with the number of firms and industries followed by the analyst. He conjectured that as an analyst's experience increases, his/her earnings forecast accuracy will increase, which implies that the analyst has a better understanding of the idiosyncrasies of a particular firm's reporting practices or he might establish a better relationship with insiders and therefore gain better access to the managers' private information. An analyst's portfolio complexity is also believed to have association with his earnings forecast accuracy. He hypothesizes that forecast accuracy will decrease with the number of firms followed. The effect of available resources impacts analyst's earnings forecast in such a way that analysts employed by larger broker firm supplies more accurate forecasts than smaller ones. The rationale behind this hypothesis is that analyst hired by a large brokerage firm has better access to the private information of managers at the companies he follows. Large firms have more advanced networks that allow the firms to better disseminate their analyst's views into the capital markets.

Testing of Hypotheses

To examine what factors influence analysts' earnings forecast for the U.S. firms issuing IPOs, several hypotheses are to be tested by using the standardized mean (median) forecast errors. The factors to be considered are: year, trading location, number of analysts providing the earnings guidance, capitalization of the firm and the sector.

A. Forecast Errors and Trading Location

The New York Stock Exchange (NYSE), the largest equity marketplace in the world, is home to about 3,000 companies worth nearly $16 trillion in global market capitalization. These companies include a cross-section of leading U.S. companies. They are well-established and have fairly stable performance. Thus, financial analysts should find their earnings relatively predictable. Therefore, the accuracy of analysts' corporate earnings forecasts for the companies listed on the NYSE should be superior to other type of markets, such as NASDAQ.

In contrast, NASDAQ is the world's largest electronic stock market; it transmits real-time quote and trade data for more than 1.3 million users in eighty-three countries. There are nearly 4,100 NASDAQ-listed securities, representing the world's leading companies. However, trading on the NASDAQ is less regulated than on the NYSE, and the NASDAQ is dominated by large institutional investors. It is also characterized by more speculative activity. Thus, one might conjecture that this market is both more volatile and less predictable than the NYSE. However, there was considerable over optimism about the NASDAQ traded IPOs. Thus, the following null hypothesis can be postulated:

H1: The accuracy of the analysts' earnings forecasts for the NYSE companies are the same as the accuracy of the NASDAQ traded companies.

The rationale being that a well-informed analyst should be able forecast earnings with the same degree of accuracy no matter where the stock is trading.

B. Forecast Errors and Year

If the predictability of earnings is stable, then there should be no difference in forecast accuracy across the three years. But the economy is neither static nor equally predictable over time. In particular, 1999 was called "the year of the IPOs." However, in 2000 and 2001 the economy started to slide into recession, and stock prices declined significantly. Consequently, the issuance of IPO slowed after March 2000 recovering to some extent only in the last couple of years. Thus, the following null hypothesis can be postulated:

H2: There is no difference among the forecast errors in 1999, 2000, and 2001.

C. Forecast Errors and the Number of Analysts

According to the forecast combination literature, the number of analysts forecasting a stock's earnings should play a significant role in the accuracy of earnings forecast. Assuming some diversity of opinion, as the number of analysts' increases, so also does the accuracy of earnings forecasts. Hence, the following null hypothesis can be postulated:

H3: There is no relationship between the forecast errors and the number of analysts forecasting the stock's earnings.

D. Forecast Errors and the Size of a Company

This study assumes that there is a direct relationship between the analysts' forecast errors and the size of a company. Larger firms, as suggested by Bhushan (1989), and Hung and Cheng (2001), are followed by more analysts with higher motivation and more financial incentive. Based on this rationale, the following hypothesis is introduced for testing:

H4: The forecast errors are unrelated to the market capitalization of the firm's equity.

Data Source and Methodology

This paper studies the accuracy of the IPO earnings forecasts conducted by financial analysts in the United States. The resources of earnings forecast data are mainly drawn from the I/B/E/S database maintained by Thomson Financial. This was supplemented from websites such as MS Money Central, Yahoo Finance, SEC Web page, First Call.com, and *Zack's Investment*. The list of the IPOs was taken from Thomson Financial database. Financial data about these companies were collected from the *Compustat* database. The years covered by our study were 1999-2001—the crucial years of IPO growth and decline.

As for methodology, we have used the summary statistics of standardized mean (median) Forecast Errors, Ordinary Least Square method, and the Multiple Regression method, in order to analyze and compare the accuracy of financial analysts' earnings forecasts.

A. Standardized Mean Forecast Errors

Let FE_{ijt} be the earnings forecast for the firm i by the analyst j at time t, then the mean earnings forecast, MFE_{it}, for the firm i at the time t, , is:

$$MFE_{it} = \frac{1}{N} \sum_{j=1}^{N} FE_{ijt}$$

(1)

where N is the number of analysts covering the firm at that time. The standardized mean forecast errors, SFE_{it} are computes as the following:

$$SFE_{it} = \frac{MFE_{it} - AE_{it}}{AE_{it}} \qquad (2)$$

where $AE_{it\ is}$ the actual earnings for the firm i at the time t, i = 1, 2, 3...
N (no of firms). The resulting data is a cross-sectional time series.

B. Regression Models

The regression models proposed here examines the dependence
of standardized forecast errors on a number of firm and trading characteristics. The independent variables tested in this study are: trading location, year, number of analysts, firm size, and the sector. First,
we test these dependent variables one at a time then jointly. These
resulting equations are:

$$SFE = \alpha + \sum_{k=1}^{2} \beta_{Tr,k} TRADE_k + \varepsilon \qquad (3)$$

where $TRADE_1$ is NASDAQ, $TRADE_2$ is NYSE. This equation will
test hypothesis 1 proposed in the earlier section. The second hypothesis is tested using the equation:

$$SFE = \alpha + \sum_{k=1}^{3} \beta_{Y,k} YEAR_k + \varepsilon \qquad (4)$$

Where $YEAR_1$ is 1999, $YEAR_2$ is 2000 and $YEAR_3$ is 2001. The
Third hypothesis is tested using the equation:

$$SFE = \alpha + \sum_{k=1}^{5} \beta_{NA,k} ANALYST_k + \varepsilon \qquad (5)$$

where $ANALYST_k$ (k=1,2...5) represent: 5 or fewer analysts, 6 to 10
analysts, 11 to 15 analysts, 16 to 20 analysts and more than 20 analysts respectively.

$$SFE = \alpha + \sum_{k=1}^{4} \beta_{SZ,k} SIZE_k + \varepsilon \qquad (6)$$

where $SIZE_k$ (k=1,2,3,4) represent market capitalization based
quartiles. Firms were ranked on the basis of their market capitalization and divided into quartiles, $SIZE_1$ being the largest. The fifth
hypothesis is tested using the equation:

$$SFE = \alpha + \sum_{k=1}^{8} \beta_{ST,k} SECTOR_k + \varepsilon \tag{7}$$

where $SECTOR_k$ the firms sector classification.

The following multiple-regression used to determine the determinants of forecast accuracy:

$$SFE = \alpha + \sum_{k=1}^{2} \beta_{Tr,k} TRADE_k + \sum_{k=1}^{3} \beta_{Y,k} YEAR_k + \sum_{k=1}^{5} \beta_{NA,k} ANALYST_k$$

$$+ \sum_{k=1}^{4} \beta_{SZ,k} SIZE_k + \sum_{k=1}^{8} \beta_{ST,k} SECTOR_k + \varepsilon \tag{8}$$

where b_{Tr}, b_Y, b_{NA}, b_{SZ}, and b_{ST} are the beta-coefficients associated with trading location, year, number of analysts, firm size, and the sector, respectively.

Empirical Findings

In table 9.1, we have given the summary statistics of the average of standardized earnings forecast error and the average of the coefficient of variation by the years 1999-2001 and by both the New York Stock Exchange and the NASDAQ stock exchange. The standardized median forecast error is the median forecast error over analysts' forecast of a given company at a given target date, divided by

Table 9.1
Summary Statistics of the Standardized Earnings Forecast Errors

A. Average of Standardized Median Forecast Errors

	NYSE		NASDAQ		Both Exchanges	
Year	Median Forecast Error	# Sample	Median Forecast Error	# Sample	Median Forecast Error	#Sample
1999	0.052	146	-0.067	58	0.018	204
2000	0.001	888	-0.097	697	-0.042	1,585
2001	-0.036	110	-0.064	95	-0.049	205
		1,144		850		1,994

B. Average Coefficient of Variation

	Coefficient of Variation	# Sample	Coefficient of Variation	# Sample	Coefficient of Variation	#Sample
1999	-0.117	146	-0.094	58	-0.110	204
2000	0.026	888	-0.068	697	-0.0151	1,585
2001	0.031	110	-0.105	95	-0.032	205
		1,144		850		1,994

the realized earnings. Here in panel A of table 9.1 we find no consistent pattern of standardized median forecast error among the years and between the two exchanges. While it was positive in the NYSE for 1999 and 2000, it was negative in 2001. But it was negative in NASDAQ for all the years covered by our study. When we combine the median forecasting error for the two exchanges, it was positive for 1999, but negative for both 2000 and 2001.

In panel B of table 9.1, we have given the average coefficient of variation by year and stock exchange. The coefficient of variation is defined as the standard deviation of the standardized forecasts of expected earnings for a given company at a given date divided by the median over forecasts. Here, also, there was no consistent pattern among the years for the NYSE, although it was negative for all the years for NASDAQ and it was true for the both combined.

In table 9.2, we have tested the null hypothesis that there is no relationship between standard forecast error and the trading location, by the ordinary least-square analysis. The standardized forecast error (FE) is the actual earnings less median forecast earnings divided by the actual earnings. Here the t-statistics for both the variables are significant at the 0.01 percent level, and P-values are approximately zero. The b-coefficient indicates that the standardized forecast error on the NASDAQ is significantly positive, showing a tendency to underforcast. The NYSE also underforcast earnings, but significantly less (0.814-0.726 = 0.088 standardized percentage points). Here the null hypothesis is rejected, since the forecast error for the NYSE, while still positive, is lower than that of the NASDAQ.

Table 9.2
Relation Between Standardized Forecast Errors and Trading Location

$$SFE = \alpha + \sum_{k=1}^{2} \beta_{Tr,k} \, TRADE_k + \varepsilon$$

	B-Coefficient	t-Stat.	P-value
NASDAQ	0.814	6.160*	0.000
NYSE	-0.726	-4.161*	0.000

* Significant at the 0.01 percent level.

Table 9.3 shows the relationship between the forecast error and the years covered by our study (1999-2001). Here the intercept represents the value of the average standardized forecast in 1999. We find that, while the b-coefficient for the intercept is significant at the 0.05 percent level, the b-coefficients for 2000 and 2001 were not significant at any level. Thus the null hypothesis is not rejected at the conventional significance level (e.g., p< 0.05). There were differences between the forecast errors in 1999, 2000, and 2001.

Table 9.4 shows the relationship between the forecast error and the number of analysts forecasting a stock's earnings. We find that

Table 9.3
Relation Between Standardized Forecast Errors and the Years

$$SFE = \alpha + \sum_{k=1}^{3} \beta_{Y,k} YEAR_k + \varepsilon$$

	B-Coefficient	t-statistic	P-value
Year 1999	0.356	1.315*	0.189
Year 2000	0.077	0.077	0.789
Year 2001	-0.195	-0.510	0.610

*Significant at the 0.05 percent level.

Table 9.4
Relationship Between the Forecast Error and the Number of Analysts

$$SFE = \alpha + \sum_{k=1}^{5} \beta_{NA,k} ANALYST_k + \varepsilon$$

A. Regression Statistics

	B-Coefficient	t-statistic	P-value
Analysts 21 or More	0.034	0.089	0.929
Analysts 16 to 20	-0.258	-0.834	0.405
Analysts 11 to 15	-0.372	-1.352**	0.177
Analysts 6 to 10	0.015	0.070	0.944
5 or less Analysts	0.465	3.386*	0.001

B. Implied Forecast Error by Number of Analysts

Number of Analysts	Forecast Error
Analysts 21 or More	0.499
Analysts 16 to 20	0.207
Analysts 11 to 15	0.093
Analysts 6 to 10	0.480
Analysts 5 or Fewer	0.465

* Significant at the 0.01 percent level.
** Significant at the 0.05 percent level.

the null hypothesis is rejected, for there is a statistically significant relationship at the 0.001 percent level (e.g., p<.002) between media forecast error and the number of analysts (for five or fewer analysts). Also, there seems to be an optimum number of analysts between eleven to fifteen as the t-statistic is significant at the 0.05 percent level. However, the t-value is not significant beyond that number, as was the number of less than eleven analysts. The forecast error shown in panel B of table 9.4 also bears that out where the error was lowest when the number of analysts was between eleven and fifteen.

In table 9.5, we have shown the relationship between the market capitalization of a company's equity and the forecast error. We find that there is a statistically positive relationship between market capitalization and forecast error for the lowest quartile of firms (p= 0.093 level), as represented by the intercept, the only other quartile which is significantly higher than the lowest quartile is the second quartile (p= 0.002 level), where the t-value is also the highest. Thus the null hypothesis, that there is no relationship between the market capitalization of a company's equity and the forecast error, is to be rejected.

Table 9.6 summarizes the results of the least-square regression analysis for nine industries surveyed. Except for the health care industry, the b-coefficients were less than 1.0, indicating that the analysts were biased toward over-estimating the earnings. In the health care industry, on the other hand, they were biased toward underestimating the earnings. But the t-values for the b-coefficients were significant only for the service, health care, and technology indus-

Table 9.5

Relationship Between the Forecast Errors and the Firm's Market Capitalizations

$$SFE = \alpha + \sum_{k=1}^{4} \beta_{SZ\,k}\, SIZE_k + \varepsilon$$

	B-Coefficient	t-statistic	P-value
Size 1	0.018	0.072	0.942
Size 2	0.746	3.060	0.002
Size 3	-0.330	-1.354	0.176
Size 4	0.289	1.679	0.093

where: Size 1 = 1 if the market capitalization is the first quartile of firms, 0 otherwise; Size 2 = 1 if the market capitalization is in the second quartile of firms, 0 otherwise; Size 3 = 1 if the market capitalization is in the third quartile of firms, 0 otherwise.

Table 9.6

Relationship Between the Forecast Error and the Firm's Industry Classification

$$SFE = \alpha + \sum_{k=1}^{9} \beta_{S,I,k} INDUSTRY_k + \varepsilon$$

	B-coefficient	t-statistic	P-value
Consumer Noncyclical	-0.340	-0.617	0.538
Service	0.470	1.909	0.056
Financial	-0.259	-0.638	0.523
Energy and Utilities	-0.048	-0.447	0.655
Transportation	-0.313	-0.278	0.781
Consumer Cyclical	-0.326	-0.876	0.381
Health Care	1.559	3.660	0.000
Basic Material & Capital Goods	-0.038	-0.651	0.515
Technology	-0.362	-1.341	0.180
Nonsurvivors (intercept)	0.325	1.743	0.081

Table 9.7

Relationship Between Forecast Errors and all the Other Prior Variables

$$SFE = \alpha + \sum_{k=1}^{2} \beta_{Tr,k} TRADE_k + \sum_{k=1}^{3} \beta_{Y,k} YEAR_k + \sum_{k=1}^{5} \beta_{NA,k} ANALYST_k$$
$$+ \sum_{k=1}^{4} \beta_{SZ,k} SIZE_k + \sum_{k=1}^{8} \beta_{ST,k} SECTOR_k + \varepsilon$$

	B-Coefficient	t-statistic	P-value
Intercept	0.666	1.979**	0.048
NYSE	-0.595	-3.210*	0.001
2000	0.013	0.043	0.965
2001	-0.348	-0.907	0.364
Analysts 21 or More	0.017	0.038	0.969
Analysts 16 to 20	-0.296	-0.823	0.411
Analysts 11 to 15	-0.643	-0.206	0.039
Analysts 6 to 10	-0.071	-0.328	0.743
Size 1	0.108	0.343	0.743
Size 2	0.937	3.562*	0.000
Size 3	-0.208	-0.849	0.396

*Significant at the 0.01 percent level.
** Significant at the 0.05 percent level.

tries. The most over-estimation of earnings forecasts took place in technology, being the most prominent industry in the IPO boom period. It is interesting to note here that the nonsurvivor firms did not have significant forecasting errors than the survivor firms.

In table 9.7, we have calculated the multiple regression equation, with forecasting error as the dependent variable and all the other variables taken in previous equations as the independent variables. Here we find that the b-coefficients of this table confirm most of the results obtained in prior simple regression equations. For the trading location, the forecast error for the NYSE is lower than the NASDAQ, thus confirming the result in the simple regression. As for the years, there is no statistically significant difference in forecast error by year, thus contradicting the result obtained in table 9.2. The number of analysts is also significant when they are between eleven and fifteen analysts. Finally, the forecast error for the second quartile is significantly higher than for the other quartiles of market capitalization, as was found in table 9.5.

Conclusion

Thus the forecasts errors by the analysts were lower for the NYSE than for the NASDAQ. There was a significant difference in analysts' forecasts for the years, which was true for the trading locations. The number of analysts between eleven and fifteen was ideal as the forecasting error in that group was the lowest. As for the forecasting errors and market capitalization, firms belonging to 25 percent to 50 percent of the group had the strongest association with the forecasting errors. Analysts were mostly biased toward overestimating the earnings of the companies than the other way around.

References

Bartley, Jon W. and Cameron, Alex B.; "Long-run earnings forecasts by managers and financial analysts," *Journal of Business Finance & Accounting*; Vol. 18, January 1991, p28.

Bhushan, Ravi; "Firm characteristics and analyst following," *Journal of Accounting & Economics*; Vol. 11, July, 1989, p. 255-274.

Clement, Michael B.; "Analyst forecast accuracy: do ability, resources, and portfolio complexity matter?" *Journal of Accounting & Economics*; Vol. 27, 1999, p.285-303.

Das, S., Levine, Carolyn B., and Sivaramakrishnan, K.; "Earnings predictability and bias in analysts' earnings forecasts," *The Accounting Review*; April, 1998, p. 277-294.

Fan-Ning, Jean and Srivastava Suresh; "Analysts' Corporate Earnings Forecast Accuracy: A Study of Year 2001." working paper, presented at the *Western Decision Science* annual meeting, April 2003.

Hung, Ken & Cheng, Weiming (2001); "Comparison of management and analyst' corporate earnings forecast: Taiwanese equity market experience," working paper, *Department of Business Management, National Donghwa University*; 2001.

Higgins, Huong Nago; "Analyst forecasting performance in seven countries," *Association for Investment Management and Research*; May/June, 1998, p.58-62.

Jaggi, B, "Further evidence on the accuracy of management forecasts vis-à-vis analyst' forecasts," The Accounting Review, January 1980, p.96-101.

Kross, W. , Ro, B. and Schreoder, D.; "Earnings expectations: the analysts information advantage," *The Accounting Review*; April 1990, p.461-476.

Orie, E. Barron, Charles, O. Kile, and Terrence, B. O'Kcelo; "MD&A quality as measured by the SEC and analysts' earnings forecasts," *Contemporary Accounting Research*; Spring, 1999, p. 75-109.

10

Summary and Conclusions

Summary of the Study

The role of the IPOs was crucial in fostering economic development of the United States economy during 1990-2000. In chapter 1, we have discussed the growth of the IPOs in number and the amount of capital they raised for the new companies that floated in this decade. Here we have focused on the birth of the Internet stocks and their special place in ushering in the information-technology (IT) revolution in the world. But if 1999 was the "Year of the IPOs," then the year 2000 was also the year when the IPO bubble was burst and the whole economy went into a recession.

Chapter 2 discussed the five stages that an IPO has to go through initially: the preparation of the prospectus, selection of the lead underwriter, the road show and bookbuilding process, IPO pricing and first-day offering, and the aftermarket and lockup expiration. We have also discussed the various hypotheses adduced in finance literature to explain the initial underpricing of stocks in the IPO market. But we have found that the "quiet period" after the issuance of an IPO is not that quiet and the aftermarket is full of underwriter's activities to stabilize the IPO price. Here we may mention the recent directive of the Securities and Exchange Commission to allow the companies issuing IPOs to keep their prospectus and other activities posted in the Internet, so that the people have a better picture of the issuing company and also opening another window of transparencies for the investing public.

In chapter 3, we have found that the first-day return of the Internet IPOs was highest in 1999, as compared to the preceding years, and the following year. Also, the first-day mean excess return for the extra-hot IPOs was extremely high, but for the cold IPOs it was negative. We have also found, like Krigman et.al. in the case of general

IPOs, that the first-day gainers continued to gain and the first-day losers continued to lose over the first year.

As to the flipping activity by the institutional investors, stocks with high flipping ratios were held the least amount and stocks with the low flipping ratios were held the maximum by the institutional investors. Both the number and the percentage of institutional shares were lowest for the cold IPOs and highest for the extra-hot IPOs, indicating that flipping was an important predictor of future performance of the IPO stocks.

When we employed the multiple regression equations in order to find the association between the return statistics on the one hand, and the relevant independent variables on the other, we have found that only the first-day opening price was significantly associated with the return variable, although the relationship was uniformly negative. But the offer price as well as the shares offered have no systematic relationship with returns, which was also true for market capitalization. Also, the low value of R^2 reflect rather weak association of these chosen variables as predictors of the IPO returns.

In chapter 4, we have found that, although the mean first-day return jumped from 3.29 percent in 1990 to 76.61 percent in 2000, the mean second-day and third-day returns were negative during the same period in the NASDAQ market. During 1990-1995, the mean post-issue one-month return was 1.67 percent, mean six-month return was 4.28 percent, and mean one-year return was 5.23 percent, respectively. This could be compared with the results for the 1996-2000 period when the mean one-month return 3.29 percent, mean six-month return was 16.96 percent, and mean one-year return was 19.97 percent, respectively. All this indicates that speculative fervor occurred on the first day of the IPO issues as compared to the subsequent days, and that 1996-2000 constituted the exception years for the NASDAQ IPOs as compared to the previous years.

As to the operating efficiency of the NASDAQ IPOs in our sample, mean inventory turnover was much higher in 2000 in comparison of 1990, but both the fixed asset turnover and working capital turnover were lower in 2000 as compared to 1990. The same decline was true for net income per employee and net income per dollar of gross plant and equipment when they were negative in 2000 in comparison of 1990. The average EPS, which was slightly negative in 1990 went down much further in 2000. As to the debt/asset ratio, it increased considerably in 1996-2000 as compared to 1990-1995, but the debt/equity ratio dipped modestly during the same comparative periods. This clearly shows that the NASDAQ "bubble" was mainly created by the equity issues, not by the issuance of debt securities. Using the multiple regression equations, we also have found that the first-day closing price was consistently and negatively associated with the annual returns. Obviously, the phenomenon of initial underpricing played a big role in determining the annual return of the NASDAQ IPOs during the last decade in the U.S. securities markets.

In chapter 5, we have found that during 1996-2000, the first-day return of NYSE IPOs was 11.97 percent, while for the NASDAQ IPOs without Internet, it was 63.33 percent, and for the Internet IPOs it was a whopping 90.28 percent, resulting in the first-day return for all IPOs to be 15.24 percent. But the one-year return for all IPOs it was a very modest 3.23 percent, and for the NASDAQ IPOs, it was 11.49 percent for that "bubble" period of the IPO history.

When we divide the return statistics into "cold," "cool," "hot" and "very hot" IPOs, we find that the first-day return for "cold" IPOs was negative throughout the different time periods. For the "cold" IPOs, except for the third-day return, it was modestly positive. But for the "hot" IPOs, it was high for all the time periods, and for "very hot" IPOs, it was extremely high for all the time periods calculated in our study. In all, average one-year mean return for "cold" IPOs was −49.18 percent, while for "hot" IPOs it was 32.93 percent in the 1990-2000 decade.

For the calendar year returns of the IPOs of our sample, we have found that in 1990, the mean return of NYSE IPOs was 20.68 percent, but for the NASDAQ IPOs, it was −18.08 percent, resulting in a mean return of of 9.02 percent for all the IPOs covered by our study. In 1999, during the so-called "bubble" year, the mean return was 6.1 percent for the NYSE IPOs, 29.97 percent for the NASDAQ IPOs, and 23.05 percent for all IPOs combined. But in 2000, they all came down considerably, being 1.37 percent for all NYSE IPOs, -64.37 percent for the NASDAQ IPOs, and −34.55 percent for all IPOs of our sample. In all, average one-year mean return for "cold" IPOs was −49.18 percent, while for "hot" IPOs it was 32.93 percent during the last decade.

As for operating efficiency, the mean operating ratio for NYSE IPOs was 1.76 in 1990 which went up to 1.82 in 2000. For the NASDAQ IPOs, , on the other hand, it was 1.78 in 1990, but came down to 1.70 in 2000. For the average annual growth of cash flows during this period, the index (1990 = 100) grew to 570.56 for the NYSE IPOs in 1990, but for the NASDAQ IPOs it really jumped to 898.93 in 1999—truly a "bubble" year for the United States IPOs.

The regression results have shown consistently positive association between the first-day closing price and the return statistics. Asset size was significant for the longer period of time, as the asset leverage was significant for the shorter periods of time. Although the debt ratios were significant in four out of six equations, the signs were not consistent. And market capitalization variable was not significant in any of the equations. But the dummy variable, differentiating the firms belonging to the NYSE and NASDAQ markets, however, was significant for the longer, not the shorter, periods of time.

In chapter 6, we have found that, in general, the returns of the venture-backed IPOs were higher than the nonventure-backed IPOs. Also, the first-day returns of both these types of IPOs were higher than any other time periods, thus buttressing the findings of other researchers that IPOs of the United States had suffered from initial underpricing. As for operating ratios of these two groups as performance measure, the results were mixed and we have not detected any clear pattern in this regard. But the growth rates of cash flows were much higher for venture-backed IPOs than the nonventure-backed IPOs during 1990-2001.

When we run the regression equations to gauge the causal relationship between return statistic as dependent variable and other relevant variables as independent variables, we find that only the first-day closing price was significantly and negatively associated with most return variables. Both market capitalization and offer price as explanatory variables were significant only in a very limited number of equations, while number of shares as explanatory variable was not significant at all in most equations. Our results thus confirm the conclusion reached by Brav and Gompers that venture-backed IPOs performed better than nonventure-backed IPOs during the period covered by our study (1990-2001).

In chapter 7, we have found that, for both the venture-backed and the nonventure-backed *Internet* IPOs, the first-day returns were much higher as compared to the second-day and third-day returns, but the first-day return of the nonventure-backed IPOs was slightly higher than that of the venture-backed IPOs. Also, both the six-month and one-year returns of the nonventure-backed IPOs were positive, while they were negative for the venture-backed IPOs. The first-day high returns, thus, support of the findings of other researchers that the IPOs of the United States had suffered from initial underpricing, which was especially true for the *Internet* IPOs. As for the operating ratios of these two groups as a performance measure, the mean operating ratios were positive during 1996-2001 for the venture-backed IPOs, except for 1997, while they were positive throughout the whole period for the nonventure-backed IPOs. Also, the annual growth of cash flows was much higher for the nonventure-backed IPOs as compared to the venture-backed IPOs during 1996-2001.

When we employ the regression equations to estimate the causal relationship between the return statistics as the dependent variable and other relevant variables as the independent variables, we find that only the first-day closing price was significantly and negatively associated with all the return variables. Offer price was also significant and negatively related, but not in all equations, while the number of shares offered as well as market capitalization were significant only in two or three equations. The negative significance of the first-day closing price in the regression results proves, again, the underpricing of the IPOs, as seen in many other studies. But our study has reached the opposite conclusion of Professors Brav and Gompers, as we find that the nonventure-backed *Internet* IPOs performed better than the venture-backed Internet IPOs when 1996-2001 period was taken into account.

In chapter 8, we have seen that the average gross spread of the United States underwriters for The IPOs during 1990-1999 was not exactly 7 percent, contrary to many other findings. It moved within the range of 5.73 percent to 9.36 percent for the IPOs listed in the NYSE, 7.24 percent to 11.06 percent for the NASDAQ IPOs, and 6.84 percent to 10.52 percent for the Internet IPOs during the period covered by our study. The average gross spread for both the markets was 8.32 percent during 1990-1999. The average offer price also fluctuated quite a bit during the period—from a range of $27.33 to $73.75 for the IPOs listed in the NYSE, from $9.30 to $30.87 for the NASDAQ IPOs, and $10.57 to $23.56 for the Internet IPOs, averaging $32.83 for the two markets combined during 1990-1999.

We have also seen that the high price of filing price range declined considerably from 1980-1989 to 1995-1999, while the low price of the filing range dipped slightly during the same period. The primary shares filed as a percentage of primary shares offered was more than halved in the later two sub-periods as compared to the earlier period. Also, the issues priced within the filing range fell slightly in 1995-1999 as compared to 1980-1989. The underwriter fees as percentage of principal amount had remained virtually unchanged from 1970-1979 to 1980-1989, and dipped slightly during 1990-1999. While the percentage of insider shares decreased considerably from 1980-89 to 1990-99, the percentage of shares in lock-up increased dramatically from 1980-89 to 1990-1990.

The multiple regression equations show that gross spread as the dependent variable was negatively and significantly associated with common equity and days in lock-up in the New York Stock Exchange, with ROA and offer price for the NASDAQ market, and no significant association with any independent variable in the Internet IPO market. The offer price as the dependent variable, although negatively and significantly associated with common equity and total debt, was positively and significantly associated with market capitalization and revenues for the IPOs in the NYSE. The offer price for the IPOs in the NASDAQ market was positively and significantly associated with the book value, the market value, ROA, ROE, and the percent of insider shares, while negatively and significantly associated with gross spread, NIAT and days in lock-up. The offer price for the Internet IPOs was positively and significantly associated with the book value, EBIT and market value of assets, but was negatively and significantly associated with NIAT during the period covered by our study.

In chapter 9, we have found that the forecasts error by the analysts was lower for the NYSE as compared to the NASDAQ—the results borne out to be true in the multiple regression models. But there was a significant difference in the forecasts errors in 1999, 2000, and 2001, contradicting the result obtained in the multiple regression equations. As the result in the simple regression was statistically more robust than the multiple regression results, we tend to support the view that trading location did make a difference in analysts' forecasting. This conclusion was also reached by Fan-Ning and Srivastava (2003) in their study of forecasts errors by the analysts.

As for the forecasts errors and the number of analysts, we find that the number between eleven and fifteen to be ideal, as the forecast error in this group was the lowest. This was also buttressed by the multiple regression results. Similarly, regarding forecast error and the size of the company as measured by market capitalization, we find that firms belonging to the second quartile (between 25 percent and 50 percent), had the strongest association with the forecast error. This was also supported by the results obtained by the multiple regression model. Finally among the industries surveyed, analysts were mostly biased toward over-estimating the earnings, except for the health care industry where they were biased toward under-estimating the earnings of the companies concerned.

In a nutshell: our study has found that the average first-day return for the NYSE-listed and NASDAQ-listed IPOs was over 15 percent during 1999-2000. It was very high for the "hot" IPOs, while negative for the "cold" IPOs. For the Internet IPOs, the first-day mean return for the extra-hot IPOs was extremely high, but for the cold IPOs it was also negative. For the NASDAQ IPOs, although the mean first-day return was very high, the mean second-day return and third-day returns were negative during 1990-2000. The first-day closing price was negatively associated with the annual returns in most of the regression analysis.

As to the pricing and long-run performance of the venture-backed and nonventure-backed IPOs, the first-day returns were much higher than any other time periods, and the returns of the venture-backed IPOs were higher than the nonventure-backed IPOs. But when we take the Internet IPOs into account, the returns of the nonventure-backed IPOs were slightly higher than that of the venture-backed IPOs. Here also, only the first-day closing price was significantly and negatively associated with most return statistics.

For the gross spread of the underwriters for the IPOs, it was not exactly 7 percent but was 8.32 percent on average for the NYSE and NASDAQ markets combined during 1990-2000. As for the analysts' forecast error of earnings, it was lower for the NYSE IPOs than the NASDAQ-listed IPOs. Also the number of analysts between eleven and fifteen was ideal as the forecast error in that group was the lowest. Finally, analysts were mostly biased toward overestimating the earnings of the IPO firms than the other way round.

Whither IPOs?

The IPO market is not dead as presumed during 2001-2003, one of the worst periods in the IPO history. According to Thomson Financial, just 111 companies went public for the first time in 2001, raising a total of $39 billion in equity capital as compared to 386 companies that went public in 2002, raising an aggregate $60 billion. And in 2003, just eighty-five companies entered the IPO market and raised $15.77 billion. From 2001 to 2003, there were fewer than 100 IPOs a year on average. In contrast, there were 100 or more new stock offerings each *quarter* in the late 1990s. Two thousand four was a better year for the IPO market as 385 companies raised $60.63 billion in equity capital. The total for 2004 was the highest since 2000, when the last downturn in the securities markets began in the March of that year.

Google.com has provided the main impetus for the current IPO interest in the market when it raised $1.92 billion on August 19, 2004, and was the largest-ever U.S. auction-style IPO. But it was not the largest IPO in 2004; that distinction went to General Electric Co.'s spun-off entity Genworth Financial that raised $2.86 billion. Second was the insurer Assurant Inc. which raised $2.02 billion in February 2004. Although Google's annualized return was 126.8 percent for 2004, the highest return that year was obtained by Marchex Inc., which ended the year 223.1 percent above its offering price.

There were more gainers than losers in 2004. For the year, 63 percent of the deals were companies with reported profits. By contrast, just a quarter of the IPOs in 1999 and 2000 came from companies that had reported a profit, according to ipohome.com in Greenwich, CT. The average IPO had risen 23 percent from its offering price by 2004's end, according to the same company. That investors are coming back to the IPO market and are undertaking risks of failure, is a sure sign that the IPO market in the United States is coming back from the abyss and is finding new growth and financial opportunities in the economy.

Today's IPOs represent a more diverse cross-section of industries and involve companies that tend to be more mature with a history of profitability than the start-up companies during the IPO mania of the late 1990s. They are not the masters of a "parallel universe" where the hypervaluation of the Internet stocks had created a weird, separate world as in 1999. They had come down to the earth with a huge thud, so to speak, in 2000-2002. Today they reflect more realistic valuation of stocks, if not on the side of undervaluation. There is also an orientation to quality in the IPO market as opposed to the high speculative content that was there in 1998 or 1999.

For the entire year of 2005, however, the financial services sector was the top industry in terms of the number of IPO stocks, energy-

and power companies coming next to it. The financial services section had surpassed 2004's dominant sectors that were health care and biotechnology, according to ipohome.com. It seemed that the unprofitable early-stage drug development companies appeared to be less appealing to the prospective investors, with several companies forced to cut their offering prices sharply before they could come to the market in 2005. But the operating environment for financial services firms continued to be good, with strong earnings and good growth prospects. Also, large-scale "carve-outs" firms from established companies have taken place recently, not seen for a long time. A "carve-out" is a partial stock-market sale of a business owned by an already listed company. Recent public offering of General Electric Co.'s insurance unit Genworth Financial Inc., or the truck fleet charge-card unit Wright Express Corp. from Cendant Corp. will be the recent examples. They are generally easy to market to the prospective investors because they have stable businesses and prominent brand recognition. Overall, the number of deals as well as the dollar volume in the IPO market had fallen in 2005 as compared to 2004. The number of deals declined to 215 IPOs from 237 deals in 2004, while the dollar volume fell to $36.1 billion from $45 billion, according to Thomson Finanacial.

But, mergers and acquisitions activities had peaked up in 2005. So far 33 percent of the withdrawn stock offerings were due to merger negotiations by the IPOs, according to Dealogic, a company which tracks this kind of deal. That rate was up from 2004 when 18 percent of the withdrawn deals were because of acquisition discussions, and was also higher than 2003 when 16 percent of the deals were pulled out for that reason. However, the number of public-equity deals that have changed into acquisitions after filing paperwork with the Securities and Exchange Commission is only part of the scene. The trend is even stronger if the number of companies in the pre-filing stage that switched were counted. Deals are being made in the middle of the pre-IPO roadshows for investors, or sometimes even before. In the case of many IPOs, the sponsors of the offering seem ready to accept an acquisition over a public offering.

Another trend we see recently is that increasingly, IPO stocks are coming from companies that have been owned by private-equity investors for a year or less, according to the IPOfinancial.com, a firm that tracks new issues. It used to take three to five years for a

firm that went private to come back to the public markets after fix-
ing the problems that beset the company before. But now the turn-
around can be as little as four months, as was the case for PanAmSat.
It went private in August 2004 and filed for a new IPO in December
of that year. One thing that is noticeable is that the companies that
went private had a large amount of debt, and the IPO proceeds are
often being used to repay at least part of the debt. Also, the money
raised in the public markets is sometimes paid in part to the private-
equity firms as special dividends.

A further recent development in the IPO market is that, instead of
venture capitalists' major support, many IPOs are backed today by
large private-equity firms such as Blackstone Group or Kohlberg
Kravis Roberts & Co, who are also active in the merger- and -acqui-
sition deals in the IPO market. According to the deal-tracking firm
Dealogic, fourteen of the forty United States IPOs that came to the
market during the first quarter of 2005, or 35 percent, were backed
by large private-equity firms, compared with 34 percent during the
first quarter of 2004, and 31 percent in the final quarter of 2004. In
contrast, just seven venture capitalist-backed IPOs had started trading in the first quarter of 2005, compared with ten in the first quarter
of 2004, according to data supplied by Venture One, a research firm
owned by Dow Jones & Co. It is worth noting that at the height of
the IPO market in the first quarter of 2000, seventy deals were venture-backed. Many of the large companies coming to the IPO market are old-line cyclical industries such as chemical manufacturing,
and non-cyclical industries like rural telecom providers. In contrast,
venture capitalists have traditionally specialized in financing nascent
technology and biotechnology firms, companies that have not performed well in the current IPO market.

Also, IPO growth may come with price. History suggests that periods of growth in share sales lead to poor performance in the broader
stock market. Over the past several years, the broader market as
measured by the S&P 500-stock index has fallen on average 1.05
percent in the three-month period, following a one-month increase
in stock offerings, according to the recent research report by Credit
Suisse Group's Credit Suisse First Boston. The inverse is also true.
The market is generally up 4.64 percent in the three-month period
following a one-month decline in total share offerings. The data thus
suggests that there is a "liquidity effect"—when there is a glut of
supply, it is difficult to absorb by the market.

We also find recently that some high-profile IPOs are silent about the exchange they plan to list their shares. Of late, a few companies have filed with the SEC to go public without revealing where their shares will trade. While that is typical for small-scale or self-underwritten offerings that stand a good chance of never becoming public, the recent group of companies has included some of the markets' most-anticipated IPOs, including online search engine Google, Inc. and the investment research firm Morningstar, Inc. NASDAQ has always marketed itself as the premier destination for high-growth technology and biotechnology companies. The NYSE has sold itself on the prestige of listing on the "Big Board." Recently, the ten largest first-day gains have all taken place on the NASDAQ, while nine out of ten largest IPOs ever have been listed on the NYSE. For some IPOs, there is little choice in where to list because they do not meet the Big Board's listing requirements, since they have no revenue yet. So the competition is more acute for companies that meet the NYSE listing standards. In the future, both stock markets also face increased competition for new IPO listings from outside markets. Alternative trading platform Archipelago Holdings Inc. has teamed up with the Pacific Stock Exchange, to create ArcaEx, an all-electronic stock market that will give stiff competition to both the NYSE and the NASDAQ for the listing of IPO companies. Although the proposed merger between NYSE and Archipelago Holdings will remove that threat, other forms of all-electronic stock exchanges may emerge in the future.

Another recent development in the IPO scene is the "auction" process of selling stocks to the public, popularized by Google, Inc. In traditional IPO selling, the Wall Street underwriters set the number and price of the stocks to be sold. With an auction, on the other hand, the investors help set the price in a bidding—the highest price that will fill all the orders is chosen, although the bankers and the company involved may agree on a discount. Besides Google, Alibris Inc., an online retailer of used or hard-to-find books, have used the auction approach to sell stock to the public for the first time. It is interesting to note that while Google is a highly profitable company, Alibris is not profitable at all. If a small company like Alibris can sell shares successfully through the auction process, then surely it will be followed by many such companies whose profit potential lies are far on the horizon. That had happened in the case of Morningstar, Inc., which in May 2005 followed the auction process successfully.

However, auctions do seem to be gaining ground, and not just for the IPOs. In May of 2004, online retailer Overstock.com Inc. sold 1.5 million shares of its stock in a follow-on issue placed through an auction, led by W.R. Hambrecht & Co. It marked the first time a secondary or follow-on sale took place in an auction. But still auction process is a rare phenomenon in Wall Street today. In 2004, three out of 251 U.S. IPOs, used the auction method.

The regulatory pressure on the investment banks is also a recent development. Regulatory action against some investment banking firms over some IPO practices, and the conflicts of interest between investment bankers and research analysts employed by the same firms had revealed that IPOs were used by investment banks as an enticement for future investment banking businesses. Company executives were offered shares in "hot" IPOs in exchange for the promise of future banking contracts from those executives. Such a practice known as "spinning" has been banned.

Similarly, the "laddering" practice has come under scrutiny by the SEC. It was found that some securities firms had doled out shares to investors based partly on their commitments to buy additional shares after trading began. This was called "laddering" of stocks sold in initial public offerings. Steering "hot" IPOs to big investors who signaled plans to buy additional shares could have stimulated additional demand for technology stocks during the stock market "bubble" of the late 1990s. It contributed to the huge first-day price gains that eventually worsened losses suffered by small investors who, lacking access to the actual IPOs, bought on the open market after trading began. If this practice is discontinued, it would create a healthier atmosphere for investment in IPOs by small investors.

Although the Sarbanes-Oxley Act of 2002 created more governmental restrictions and the ensuing costs to go public, that did not deter companies that really needed external funding from going ahead and flourish. Sarbanes-Oxley was designed to tighten governance and audit standards at publicly-traded companies in the wake of corporate bankruptcies such as Enron, Worldcom and others. Among other things, it forced company executives to personally certify financial results and placed more responsibility on corporate boards. But the IPO activity has increased since Sarbanes-Oxley went into effect. According to the Thomson Financial, in the second quarter of 2004, fifty-eight companies sold stocks to the public for the first time in the United States markets, raising $10.2 billion. For the same quarter in 2003, just five companies came to the IPO market, raising $1.8 billion. The number of companies filing with the Securities and Exchange Commission to go public had also risen considerably in 2004 from the previous three years. As one investment banker put it bluntly, "they go public because they need the capital."

But still there is a considerable financial burden for firms to bear in going public. It is being acutely felt by smaller companies that just do not have the revenues to cover the additional expenses. For companies with revenue of less than $1 billion, the cost of being a public company—including insurance, accounting and board compensation—rose 35 percent to $2.86 billion in 2003 from $2.13 billion in 2002, according to a survey done by the law firm Folay & Lardner LLP in Chicago, Illinois. The biggest cost came in areas such as directors' and officers' liability insurance, the cost of which has more than doubled since the Sarbanes-Oxley Act was passed. Since then the director compensation has nearly tripled. But for many companies, the added costs are worth bearing. For example, many bio-technology companies that came to the IPO market had little or no revenue, let alone profit. They have survived only by receiving financing from venture capitalists. For companies such as these, they go public because of their need for external capital. In the end, the decision or not go public rests less with the new costs, but rather with how high public investors are willing to value a company.

Initial public offerings (IPOs) are the main vehicle for firms to raise capital from the public who are not blessed with substantial venture capitalists' funds. It serves the useful function of capital formation and risk-taking whereby the intrepid entrepreneurs are rewarded handsomely, or are thrown into bankruptcies. At the same time, being a public company means the firm will be subject to public scrutiny and governmental regulations not encountered before. But so long as the securities markets are fair and transparent, more and more companies will go public for the first time and channel public savings into investments, thereby enriching the economy and creating employment, income and growth in the private sector.

Bibliography

Affleck-Graves, J., S. Hedge, R.E. Miller, and F. K. Reilly, 1993, "The Effect of Trading System on the Underpricing of Initial Public Offerings," *Financial Management*, 22, 99-108.

Affleck-Graves, J., S. Hedge, and R. E. Miller, 1996, "Conditional Price Trends in the Aftermarket for Initial Public Offerings," *Financial Management*, 25-40.

Allen, F., and R. G. Faulhaven, 1986, "Signaling by Underpricing in the IPO Market," *Journal of Finance*, 43, 303-323.

Aggarwal, R., 2000, "Stabilization Activities by Underwriters After New Offerings," *Journal of Finance*, 55, 1075-1104.

Aggarwal, R., and P. Conroy, "Price Discovery in Initial Public Offerings and the Role of the Lead Underwriter," *Journal of Finance*, 57, 1421-1442.

Aggarwal, R., Nagpurnanand, R. Prabhala, and M. Puri, 2002, "Institutional Allocation in Initial Public Offerings: Empirical Evidence," *Journal of Finance*, 57, 1421-1442.

Asquith, D., J. D. Jones, and R. Kieschnick, 1998, "Evidence on Price Stabilization and Underpricing in Early IPO Returns," *Journal of Finance*, 53, 1759-1773.

Barry, C. B., C. J. Muscarella, J. W. Peavy III, and M. R. Vetsuypens, 1990, "The Role of Venture Capital in the Creation of Public Companies: Evidence from the Going-Public Process," *Journal of Financial Economics*, 27, 447-471.

Benveniste, L. M., and P. A. Spindt, 1989, "How Investment Bankers Determine the Offer Price and Allocation of New Issues," *Journal of Financial Economics*, 24, 343-361.

Bradley, D. J., B. D. Jordan, and J. R. Ritter, 2003, "The Quiet Period Goes with a Bang," *Journal of Finance*, 58, 1-36.

Brav, A., and P. A. Gompers, 1997, "Myth or Reality? The Long-Run Underperformance of Public Offerings: Evidence from Venture and Non-Venture Capital-Backed Companies," *Journal of Finance*, 52, 1791-1821.

Brav, A., 2000, "Inference in Long-Horizon Event Studies: A Bayesian Approach with Application to Initial Public Offerings," *Journal of Finance*, 55, 1979-2016.

Carter, R. B., F. H. Dark, and A. K. Singh, 1998, "Underwriter Reputation, Initial Returns, and the Long-Run Performance of IPO Stocks," *Journal of Finance*, 53, 285-311.

Cornelli, F., and D. Godreich, 2003, "Book Building: How Informative is the Order Book?" *Journal of Finance*, 58, 1415-1443.

Datta, S., M. Iskandar-Datta, and A. Patel, 1997, "The Pricing of Initial Public Offers of Corporate Straight Debt," *Journal of Finance*, 52, 379-396.

Ellis, K., R. Michaely, and M. O'Hara, 2000, "When the Underwriter is the Market Maker: An Examination of Trading in the IPO Aftermarket," *Journal of Finance*, 55, 1039-1074.

Ellis, K., R. Michaely, and M. O'Hara, 2002, "The Making of a Dealer Market: From Entry to Equilibrium in the Trading of Nasdaq Stocks," *Journal of Finance*, 57, 2289-2316.

Field, L. C., and G. Hanka, 2001, "The Expiration of IPO Share Lockups," *Journal of Finance*, 56, 471-500.

Field, L. C., and J. M. Karpoff, 2001, "Takeover Defenses of IPO Firms," *Journal of Finance*, 57, 1857-1889.

Ghosh, A., 2003, "Post-Issue Operating Performance of Nasdaq IPOs," *Journal of Business and Economic Research*, Vol. 1, No. 1.

_____ , 2003, "Pricing and Long-Run Performance of the Venture-Backed and Nonventure-Backed IPOs," *International Business & Economic Research Journal*, 2, 87-93.

_____ , 2003, "Pricing and Performance of the United States IPOs, 1990-2000," *Journal of Accounting and Finance Research*, Vol. 11, No.4.

_____ , 2005, "The Pricing and Performance of Internet IPOs," *Advances in Financial Planning & Accounting*, (new Issue), Vol. 1, No. 1.

Grinblatt, M., and C. Y. Hwang, 1989, "Signaling and the Pricing of New Issues," *Journal of Finance*, 44, 393-420.Hanley, K. W., 1993, "The Underpricing of Initial Public Offerings and the Partial Adjustment Phenomenon," *Journal of Financial Economics*, 34, 231-250.

Hanley, K. W., and W. J. Wilhelm, 1995, "Evidence on the Stategic Allocation of Initial Public Offerings," *Journal of Financial Economics*, 37, 239-257.

Hellman, T., and M. Puri, 2002, "Venture Capital and the Performance of Start-Up Firms: Empirical Evidence," *Journal of Finance*, 58, 169-197.

Higgins, H. N., 1998, "analyst Forecasting Performance in Seven Countries," *Association for Investment Management and Research*, May-June, 58-62.

Hughes, P. J., and A. V. Thakor, 1992, "Litigation Risk, Intermediation, and the Underpricing of Initial Public Offerings," *Review of Financial Studies*, 5, 709-742.

Ibbotson, R. G., J. R. Sindelar, and J. R. Ritter, 1988, "Initial Public Offerings," *Journal of Applied Corporate Finance*, 1, 37-45.

Jain, B. A., and O. Kini, 1994, "The Post-Issue Operating Performance of IPO Firms," *Journal of Finance*, 49, 1699-1726.

Kandel, S., O. Serag, and A. Wohl, 1999, "The Demand for Stocks: An Analysis of IPO Auctions," *Review of Financial Studies*, 12, 227-248.

Krigman, L., W. H. Shaw, and K. L. Womack, 1999, "The Persistence of IPO Mispricing and the Predictive Power of Flipping," *Journal of Finance*, 54, 1015-1044.

——————————————, 2001, "Why do Firms Switch Underwriters?" *Journal of Financial Economics*, 60, 245-284.

Loughran, T., J. R. Ritter, and Rydqvist, 1994, "Initial Public Offerings: International Insights," *Pacific-Basin Finance Journal*, 2, 165-199.

Loughran, T., and J. R. Ritter, 1995, "The New Issues Puzzle," *Journal of Finance*, 50, 23-51.

——————————————, 2002, "Why Don't Issuers Get Upset about Leaving Money on the Table in IPOs?" *Review of Financial Studies*, 15, 413-443.

Lowry, M., and G. W. Schwart, 2002, "IPO Market Cycles: Bubbles or Sequential Learning?" *Journal of Finance*, 57, 1171-1200.

Megginson, W. L., and K. Weiss, 1991, "Venture Capitalist Certification in Initial Public Offerings," *Journal of Finance*, 46, 879-903.

Mello, A., and J. Parsons, "Going Public and Ownership Structure of the Firm," *Journal of Financial Economics*, 49, 79-109.

Michaely, R., and W. H. Shaw, 1994, "The Pricing of Initial Public Offerings: Tests of Adverse Selection and Signaling Theories," *Review of Financial Studies*, 7, 279-319.

Michaely, R., and K. Womack, 1999, "Conflict of Interest and the Credibility of Underwriter Analyst Recommendation," *Review of Financial Studies*, 12, 653-686.

Narasimham, J., M. Weinstein, and I. Welch, 1993, "IPO Signaling and Subsequent Equity Offerings: An Empirical Investigation," *Journal of Financial Economics*, 34, 153-176.

Orie, E., B. Charles, O.Kile, and T. B. O'Kcelo, 1999, "MD&A Quality as Measured by the SEC and Analysts' Earning Forecasts," *Contemporary Accounting Research*, Spring, 75-109.

Rajan, R., and H. Servaes, 1997, "Analyst Following of Initial Public Offerings," *Journal of Finance*, 52, 507-529.

Ritter, J. R., 1991, "The Long-Run Performance of Initial Public Offerings," *Journal of Finance*, 46, 3-27.

——————, 1998, "Initial Public Offerings," *Contemporary Finance Digest*, 2, 5-30.

Ritter, J. R., and I. Welch, 2002, "A Review of IPO Activity, Pricing, and Allocations," *Journal of Finance*, 57, 1795-1828.

Rock, K., 1986, "Why new Issues are Underpriced," *Journal of Financial Economics*, 15, 187-212.

Rund, J. S., 1993, "Underwriter Price Support and the IPO Underpricing Puzzle," *Journal of Financial Economics*, 34, 135-151,

Schultz, P., and M. Zaman, 1994, "Aftermarket Support and Underpricing of Initial Public Offerings," *Journal of Financial Economics*, 35, 199-220.

Sherman, A. E., 2000, "IPO and Long-Term Relationship: An Advantage of Book Building," *Review of Financial Studies*, 13, 697-714.

Teoh, S. H., I. Welch, and T. J. Wong, 1998, "Earnings Management and the Long-Run Market Performance of Initial Public Offerings," *Journal of Finance*, 53, 1935-1974.

Timic, S., 1988, "Anatomy of Initial Public Offerings of Common Stock," *Journal of Finance*, 43, 789-822.

Welch, I., 1989, "Seasonal Offerings, Imitation Costs, and the Underpricing of Initial Public Offerings," *Journal of Finance*, 44, 421-449.

Index

DATE DUE
